There To Breathe
THE BEAUTY

The Camping Trips of Henry Ford • Thomas Edison • Harvey Firestone • John Burroughs

There T
THE B

ART DIRECTOR: Stephen J. Tolerico
BOOK DESIGN: Identity Design Group

Breathe
EAUTY

By Norman Brauer

Norman Brauer Publications
Dalton, Pennsylvania 18414
Library of Congress Cataloging-in-Publication Data

Brauer, Norman.
There To Breathe The Beauty / written by Norman Brauer.
For information call (717) 563- 2244 or (717) 563-1888.

Acknowledgements

This work has been made possible only by many kindnesses and by the assistance of people who were sincerely interested in and committed to the successful narration of the famous camping trips.

It would be impossible to list all the people who, over the past fifteen or so years, have contributed, at least in some small way, to the project. However, I'll endeavor herewith to give credit to the major players.

My wife, Marjorie, and our sons, Barry, Robert and Benjamin, have, each in their own way, given moral support. I will be forever indebted to William Clay Ford, Raymond Firestone, Ann O. Edison and Elizabeth Burroughs Kelley for graciously signing the limited edition, and to Bob Troyer, Chicago, Illinois, for his invaluable support and assistance in coordinating the signing project. Steven Hamp and Judith Edleman guided our progress from the Henry Ford Museum and Greenfield Village, Dearborn, Michigan. Mary Gid, archivist of the Firestone Tire and Rubber Company, provided much valuable information and assistance, for which I am especially grateful. Ira Fine, Red Bank, New Jersey, lent his literary expertise in the initial editing stages. Attorney David Morgan, Jr., Dalton, Pennsylvania, kept me on track when the going became especially difficult. And finally there were John Miller, archivist of the Bierce Library, University of Akron, Akron, Ohio; Barbara Deveneau and Rich Gnatowski, Longfellow's Wayside Inn, Sudbury, Massachusetts; Dean Ross, Hanover Bank, Wilkes-Barre, Pennsylvania; Matt Allagrucci, Justus, Pennsylvania; Maryellen Calemmo, Lackawanna Historical Society, Scranton, Pennsylvania; Rosamond Peck, Waverly, Pennsylvania; and Ann O. Edison's niece, Ann (Nancy) Robbins, and her father, Harold S. Sears.

Professional Contributors

Stephen J. Tolerico, Scranton, Pennsylvania—Art Direction.

Identity Design Group, Scranton, Pennsylvania—Book Design.

Jack McDonough, Dunmore, Pennsylvania—Editing and Consultation.

Nancy Kane, Scranton, Pennsylvania—Consultation.

Ward Roe, Dalton, Pennsylvania—Consultation.

Jim Sturdevant, Waverly, Pennsylvania—Map layout.

Clement Skirpan, Throop, Pennsylvania—Final Artwork for Borders and Maps.

Fred Valentine, Llewellyn and McKane, Inc., Wilkes Barre, Pennsylvania—Printing.

Allan Geiser, Allan Geiser and Son, Philadelphia, Pennsylvania—Book Binding.

Preface

Following the First World War, the United States of America found itself, in due course, a major player on the world scene, and Americans were ready to elevate some of their heroes and heroines to superhero status. The sports world was producing its own hero-athletes, such as Ty Cobb, Jack Dempsey, Harold "Red" Grange and Babe Ruth. The business community simultaneously was bestowing the mantle of greatness on Henry Ford, Thomas Edison and Harvey Firestone, whose names had become so much a part of the public consciousness that they were already household words, in their own time: Edison for lighting homes, Ford for making the Car for Everyman, Firestone for putting tires on the cars and creating the American rubber industry.

Less famous, but perhaps more revered by those who knew him, was John Burroughs, the poet-naturalist, who devoted his life to observing and recording natural phenomena in simple, expressive terms.

This unlikely foursome, in the decade between 1915 and 1924, variously enjoyed camping by streams, touring historic rural towns, and rubbing shoulders with presidents of the United States. Each was a national figure in his own particular field. Each was accustomed to the deference which goes with leadership. Three were men of great personal wealth, used to luxury; the other reached greatness sans material wealth. Age failed them as a common bond; at the time of the first full-fledged outing by all four men, in 1918, Burroughs (born 1837) was 81; Edison (born 1847) was 71; Ford (born 1863) was 55; and Firestone (born 1868) was 50.

Had they been little men, narrow-minded, vain and selfish, their outings could have been a short-lived experiment, but the four were, in fact, close enough friends that for a period at the close of and following World War I they banded together, usually for two weeks in the summer, for a series of absolutely remarkable camping trips, outings and assorted adventures so rash and delightful that it is impossible to imagine any four such powerful and famous men duplicating the feat in this overpopulated, hyperfast, media-frenzied, stretched-out Age of Ours.

This book is an attempt to recapture, in anecdote and pictures (there are nearly 300 of them) the spirit and record of those remarkable trips during which these giants became, as witness after witness remarked, like boys again. We should note that the trips never went west of the Mississippi and three of the trips took the troupe through Vermont/New Hampshire.

Philosophers endeavoring to get at a man's real nature and character will frequently watch him at play. The effort to probe beneath the surface will usually show that the way a man works is partly due to training, theory, rules. But when a man plays, he is like a horse out of harness, free to choose and roam. The mark of a man can be partly determined by his use of freedom. Instead of loafing in chairs or touring where the roads are paved and hotels luxurious, these men struck out for the difficult, out-of-the-way mountain routes or sought an environment rich in historic lore. Usually they slept in tents, ate in the open air and at night built their own campfire, around which they sat, swapping stories under the stars.

The trips were impressively organized and equipped. There were several heavy passenger cars, flivvers and vans to carry the travelers, servants and equipment. Tents, cots and chairs were loaded into one van, while another truck was fitted out like a grocery shop with shelves and drawers for food supplies and space for stoves and ovens. On later trips they took a large, round folding table that could seat about twenty. The table was equipped with a Lazy Susan in the center.

Eggs and cream were always bought from a farmer along the route, with chickens and steaks purchased in town. Harold Sato had an expense account for handling all the food bills, and Fred Loskowski had an account for other supplies. When a trip was concluded, Ford would give them money for tickets and gasoline to see them back home to Detroit. Expense account balances always came back to Mr. Frank Campsall, Ford's personal secretary.

Camping with friends was a pleasant diversion from the everyday pressures associated with their roles as giant entrepreneurs. Inevitably, serenity would be short-lived as word got out of their pending arrival and a community turned out en masse to see the famous foursome and entreat them to speak at or add glamor to a civic meeting or local cause. The group's unpredictable route changes at forks in the road thus had their advantages: every turn that departed from the adopted itinerary sent the caravan into remote valleys and hamlets where the cloak of anonymity let them relax.

By day they motored at a leisurely pace over back roads, through mountainous, semiwild countryside. At noon they paused for lunch and toward nightfall they selected a congenial spot for a camp. Each campsite was christened with a distinctive name. While the staff was unpacking the trucks and setting up the tents, Edison settled down in his car to read or meditate, or stretched out under a tree for a nap. Ford was too active for that and scouted around, inspecting the stream and the campsite or collecting wood for the fire. Each morning and evening he took a brisk half-hour walk.

Around the campfire at night they told stories, read or talked. The inevitability of a World War ("the Huns are boneheads"–Edison) was an omnipresent subject for discussion. Each was an expert in his own field and could contribute interesting and authoritative information. Firestone expounded on solid business principles: control your supply sources, finance business expansion yourself and keep adequate cash in banks. Edison discoursed at length on chemical matters, while Ford discussed mechanical problems and Burroughs represented the literary viewpoint. Both Burroughs and Ford were well informed on bird lore, and birds and wildlife commanded much of their attention. Ford and Edison during these camping trips were intrigued by the possibilities of using waterpower to develop hydroelectric capabilities. Nary a stream was passed without their measuring the force and flow of the water, nor an abandoned mill spied without their inspecting the old waterwheels for ways to put wasted power to work.

The idea for their camping trips took root at the Pan-Pacific Exposition in San Francisco in 1915, where Ford, Edison and Firestone attended the fair's Edison Day celebration. The

Exposition was an event which marked the completion of the Panama Canal and San Francisco's rise from the rubble of the 1906 earthquake. Over the course of the next year the plans for the first outing came together, although an unexpected obligation prevented Ford from joining the troupe for the original trip; and then pressures put upon the entire industrial structure by the country's belated entrance into World War I ruled out a 1917 expedition.

By the time they parted company in 1924, after the last of the trips, the role each had assumed early on had become established through each succeeding expedition. Firestone became the "general manager" and commissary officer. Provisions were never wanting and each "safari" produced the anticipated "goodies." Firestone described Edison as the navigator, rulemaker and flower-gatherer. "He [Edison] writes us, giving the route, then he writes again, giving another route and when we actually get started, he usually selects a third route. We are kept guessing where we are going, and I suspect he does also! Complaints were lodged that Edison never chose a comfortable route if a rocky road was available.

"He rides in the front seat of the front car and directs the caravan by compass. He dislikes paved roads, and never does he select a main highway if he can find a byway. And never does he take us into a town if he can find another way around. When he thinks we have gone far enough, he decides to camp and then we camp.

"But he is not a bad leader, for he does not insist upon getting out early in the morning. The chief trouble is in getting him to bed. He likes to sit up until past midnight, talking by the campfire. And he is an exceedingly interesting talker, for not only is he a good storyteller but he has a marvelous range of information. He reads a great deal and he remembers what he reads, so that he can talk deeply on any subject. As everyone knows, he is an indomitable worker, but when he is on vacation he does not try to work. He does exactly what he pleases: he goes to bed late and rises late, and whenever there is nothing else to do, he either goes to sleep or reads a newspaper. He is lost without a newspaper!"

Ford, who was unable to accompany the famous foursome for the 1916 trip, joined up in 1918, contributed an expertise in mechanical matters that solved a number of problems for the travelers and engaged in his favorite pastime of tinkering. On one trip he saw a farmer cutting wood with a saw powered by a gas engine that was running roughly, and he repaired it. During a trip to Burroughs's home in New York State, Ford repaired a clock and remodeled a birdhouse for wrens. When the radiator on one of the touring cars was punctured by a broken fan blade, and the local garageman pronounced it beyond repair, Ford plugged the leaks.

The Ford fascination with waterpower motivated him to utilize the River Rouge in Dearborn, Michigan to provide power for the generators at his residence. A Fordson tractor plant built on Green Island tapped the Hudson River in New York State and later, while refurbishing his newly acquired Wayside Inn, Sudbury, Massachusetts, he added a gristmill on little Hop Brook. He was athletic and loved to compete, and there were contests in cradling and sheaving wheat and chopping trees, as well as footraces and target shoots.

Burroughs, the naturalist, alternated between conducting wildflower classes for Edison and sharing bird study with Ford, an avian expert in his own right. Burroughs, as an octogenarian and senior member of the group, was always accorded the "guest of honor" seating for dining, even though this might only have been next to the campfire beside a stream.

Edison was the dominant figure of the group. Although his life was centered in his laboratory, he was, nevertheless, both interested in and well versed about wonders of nature. Be they birds, flowers or stones, he knew their secrets. There seemingly was not a subject on which the great inventor could not talk intelligently. Burroughs said of Edison, "We all defer instinctively to him, he is a big-brained man, genial and good-natured. Never saw him grumpy or in ill-humor yet; also he has a big fund of stories." Yet Burroughs was the one to whom they showed gentle deference. He disagreed with Ford, philosophically, about man's using the automobile: "God designed and destined man to walk!" But it was just this divergence of views that had brought the two men together (Ford had searched out Burroughs) and ultimately made them fast friends.

Ford and Edison were "diamonds in the rough." Prep school and college training did not enter into their formal education, which consisted of limited grade-school-level work augmented, fortunately, by talented and caring mothers in their homes. Nancy Elliot Edison, a former schoolteacher, tutored her son Thomas Alva. Mary Litogot Ford taught her son Henry, and he mastered the McGuffey Reader even before entering the Scotch Settlement School in Dearborn Township, Michigan.

The lack of peer interaction and the "polish" it might have produced created difficulties for both Ford and Edison in dealing with the public in general. Their approach to elements outside their personal environment was somewhat unsophisticated, even self-conscious. Ford was very uneasy about public speaking and quite camera shy. Edison was no orator, and his hearing difficulties caused problems in social interaction. Each switched from one philosophical tenet to another; over time, however, these two giants became very adept mechanically and highly creative. Each threw himself into a creative situation and would not rest until a solution was found—frequently after days of continuous effort. Basic tenets for them were hard work and sobriety. They set high standards—both for themselves and others—and usually attained them.

Firestone and Burroughs had been fortunate enough to continue their formal education beyond the public school level. John Burroughs attended Cooperstown Academy in New York State in 1856, arriving there with enough money to last until the end of the summer term. During those three months he began studies in Latin and English literature while continuing studies in French and mathematics. Before that he had enrolled in the Hedding Literary Institute, where he studied the classics, thereby qualifying for a teaching certificate. Harvey Firestone fortuitously had a first-class high-school education at Columbiana, Ohio, and after graduating spent three months at the Spencerian Business College in Cleveland, readying himself for a business career.

John Burroughs, in the late fall of 1920, hosted his friends and their wives at Yama Farms Inn near Napanoch, New York. After a tree-chopping contest, won by Burroughs, the group was treated later on to Burroughs's famous shish kebab, broiled in an outside fireplace near his West Park, New York, residence. Despite some snow showers, the participants went along with the cookout and then retired nearby to his son Julian's home, Lovecote, where a fine buffet supper was served. This was an especially memorable time for the foursome because Burroughs died the following March at age eighty-four.

The 1921 camping trip took on grandiose aspects when the respective wives were invited along, the highlight being a weekend spent with the President of the United States, Warren G. Harding. Firestone was determined to raise hosting to a new level of excellence because an agreement to supply sixty-five percent of the tires for Henry Ford's production line was the shot in the arm he needed to combat a business downturn. From the days when he was lieutenant governor of Ohio, Warren Gamaliel Harding was a friend of Firestone's, so he readily accepted an invitation to join the campers in Maryland during July 1921. Along with the wives and the President, the entourage included one Methodist bishop, the President's secretary, several secret service agents, chauffeurs, cooks and assorted attendants, plus a plethora of journalists, cameramen and publicity agents. Also enlisted to help was Firestone's Aunt Nannie Lower and the ladies' aid society of Columbiana, Ohio, who killed, cleaned and dressed one hundred chickens and baked a mountain of cakes and cookies for the campers.

Sadness prevailed in August 1923 when the group assembled at Harding's funeral in Marion, Ohio, prior to embarking on a trip to the Upper Peninsula of Michigan. A stopover at Edison's birthplace in Milan, Ohio, where a brass band blared a greeting, brightened spirits before the group motored to Traverse City, Michigan, and boarded Henry Ford's yacht, the *Sialia* (Native American for Bluebird), for a voyage to a tenting site at Iron Mountain. Ford's vast landholdings, which included logging camps, sawmills and the Imperial Mine, were inspected, and Firestone tried out his new balloon tires to convince Ford that this was the new generation of riding comfort. Ford, who was biased toward the tried and true, was converted to using them on his production line somewhat later.

On their last joint expedition, in 1924, Henry Ford was the host at the Wayside Inn, South Sudbury, Massachusetts, an inn he had purchased a year earlier in keeping with his taste for old buildings, furniture, farm equipment and machinery. This 1686 tavern that had served the tired and thirsty travelers on the old Boston Post Road had inspired Henry Wadsworth Longfellow's "Tales of a Wayside Inn." His daughter, Alice Longfellow, graced the occasion with her presence at the inn with the Fords, Edisons and Firestones.

Ford's fascination with waterpower had prompted him to rebuild the old flour mill and its overshot waterwheel. The guests were supplied with produce from the farm, which consisted of raw milk, raw vegetables and whole-grain foods in keeping with Ford's new dietary convictions. Guests were instructed by a pair of dancing teachers in such old-fashioned dances as the Virginia reel, the varsovienne and the gavotte.

The Middlesex County Farm Bureau was treated to a picnic attended by more than three thousand locals, where an exhibition of farming methods ranged from ox teams to Ford's latest Fordson tractors.

The highlight of this trip was a junket through New England to a meeting with President Calvin Coolidge, his wife, Grace, and his father, Colonel John Coolidge, at Plymouth, Vermont. Coolidge conducted a tour of the nearby cheese factory, providing a running commentary on the cheesemaking process. The president presented his great-great-grandfather's maple sap bucket, which dated back to 1790, to Henry Ford, who later placed it on display at the Wayside Inn. Everyone present duly inscribed the bucket, and the event was recorded by the press and postcard manufacturers. A final event saw Edison present Grace Coolidge with his trusty compass, which had, in so many happy days past, led the camping party down numerous shaded country lanes and past cool, babbling brooks.

After 1924 the growing fame of the campers brought so much public notice en route that the trips were discontinued. Although the camping comrades were to meet each other again on numerous occasions, the pressures of an admiring public had taken their toll. The fun was fading and their wanderings along back roads, punctuated by their ponderings around the campfires, had come to an end.

The camping vans were preserved intact, however, and the fabulous Lazy Susan table, complete with cups, plates, silverware and chairs, was displayed for a time in the Henry Ford Room in the Henry Ford Museum in Dearborn, Michigan. At each place was the personal signature of the person who sat there at the time of President Harding's visit in 1921.

Shortly before passing away in 1921, John Burroughs summed up their happy wanderings thus: "It often seemed to me that we were a luxuriously equipped expedition going forth to seek discomfort—dust, rough roads, heat, cold, irregular hours, accidents. But discomfort, after all, is what the camper-out is unconsciously seeking—we react against our complex civilization and long to get back for a time to first principles."

A final note on sources and methodology. The principal sources for my description of the trips, and for the various quotations from visitors and bystanders, are the rather meticulous notes made daily during the excursions by Harvey Firestone and his two sons, Harvey, Jr. and Russell, who accompanied their father at various times on various trips. They kept diaries and notes, and immediately upon completion of the trips would write up an overall account.

John Burroughs was the only other member of the entourage who kept a journal, although, as was his wont, a more philosophical and poetic one, and I quote (often at length) passages from these journals.

In addition to his written record, it was Firestone who also always provided for photographers—either professionals or a member of the crew—to keep a visual record of the doings, and almost all the photographs you see here derive from those assignments, and come from the Firestone Tire and Rubber Company Archives, housed in the Bierce Library at the University of Akron. The Firestone notes, preserved in the same place, were made available to me in 1980 during my project research; many thanks to archivist Mary Gid for her assistance to me during this time. The Burroughs journals now repose in the library of Vassar College, Poughkeepsie, New York.

The photos which accompany the Burroughs Tribute come from four sources: Harvard's Theodore Roosevelt Collection (the 1903 trip); courtesy Elizabeth Burroughs Kelly (1920, Riverby and Slabsides); John Muir, *The Mountains of California*, New York, Century Company, 1894; John Burroughs, *Camping and Tramping with Roosevelt*, Houghton Mifflin Company, Boston and New York.

Firestone, based upon his notes, privately published two books about the trips, distributed only to his fellow campers and close associates. The first of these, *In Nature's Laboratory* (published 1917), covered the 1916 trip and contained tipped-in photographs and verse; the second, *Our Vacation Days of 1918* (published 1926) contained photographs and excerpts from Burroughs's journals. (I have preserved these titles, and other Firestone phrases, in titling my chapters.) Burroughs relates his 1918 trip anecdotes in his book, *Under The Maples* (published 1921), in chapter 8, "A Strenuous Holiday." A project to complete the preservation of the trips in book form died in 1931, a casualty of the Great Depression.

Norman Brauer
June 1995

DEDICATED TO:
*My Wife Margie
and My Sons Barry,
Bobby and Benjie.
Love, Dad.*

Mr. Brauer's two previous books.

Table of Contents

ABOVE: *John Burroughs, to the left of President Theodore Roosevelt, Major Pitcher and Secretary Leob, in the light coat, in Gardiner, Montana, at the start of their Yellowstone camping trip in 1903.*

Introduction
A TRIBUTE TO JOHN BURROUGHS
"The Insights and Experiences He Brought to the Camping Trips"

To Henry Ford, Thomas Edison and Harvey Firestone, John Burroughs—a friendly, intellectual, literary, poet-naturalist—was clearly one of their persuasion and being so he was invited to participate in their famous camping trips and vacations around the countryside. Burroughs was in his early eighties as he accompanied them from 1916 to 1920. This man of letters was loved and respected by all who knew him. Professors, scholars, writers and clergymen comprised a select group of intelligentsia who were privileged to share his understanding of nature's phenomena. This Tribute is an attempt to give the reader a better understanding of the man.

Firestone's book covering their 1918 trip was dedicated to Burroughs, who had passed away in March 1921. Firestone wrote:

"John Burroughs, by his own life, as well as by his pen, led mankind into the open and to an appreciation of the beauty of the natural. And so we find him as a compatriot—a congenial companion of the outdoors, a philosopher who worshipped God's truth in nature—a life based on simple sane living. Mr. Burroughs has written the story in this book, which gives an insight into the man himself, as well as an account of our travels. To his memory this book is dedicated."

The book's frontispiece contained a quote from Burroughs, which was apropos:

> To the woods and fields or to the hills
> There to breathe their beauty like the very air
> To be not a spectator of, but a participator in, it all!

Burroughs also published his account of the 1918 camping trip entitled, "A Strenuous Holiday," in his 1921 book, *Under The Maples*. The beginning lines reveal a marvelous, colorful, idiosyncratic style that is appealing even to the most critical eye.

"One August a few years ago (1918) I set out with some friends for a two weeks' automobile trip into the land of Dixie—joy-riders with a luxurious outfit calculated to be proof against any form of discomfort.

"We were headed for the Great Smokey Mountains in North Carolina. I confess that mountains and men that do not smoke suit me better. Still I can stand both, and I started out with the hope that the great Applachian range held something new and interesting for me. Yet I knew it was a risky thing for an octogenarian to go a-gypsying, and with younger men. Old blood has lost some of its red corpuscles, and does not warm up easily over the things that moved one so deeply when one was younger. More than that, what did I need of an outing? All the latter half of my life has been an outing, and an "inning" seemed more in order. Then, after fourscore years, the desire for change, for new scenes and new people, is at low ebb. The old and familiar draw more strongly. Yet I was fairly enlisted and bound to see the Old Smokies."

As the senior member of the group, Burroughs had spent a lifetime pursuing the very essence of nature. An examination of the following list of books that he penned proves this point. To wit: *Notes on Walt Whitman as Poet and Person*, 1867; *Wake-Robin*, 1871; *Winter Sunshine*, 1875; *Birds and Poets*, 1877; *Locusts and Wild Honey*, 1879; *Pepacton*, 1881; *Fresh Fields*, 1884; *Signs and Seasons*, 1886; *Indoor Studies*, 1889; *Riverby*, 1894; *Whitman, A Study*, 1896; *The Light of Day*, 1900; *Literary Values*, 1902; *The Life of Audubon*, 1902; *Far and Near*, 1904; *Ways of Nature*, 1905; *Bird and Bough* (poems), 1906; *Camping and Tramping with Roosevelt*, 1907; *Leaf and Tendril*, 1908; *Time and Change*, 1912; *The Summit of the Years*, 1913; *The Breath of Life*, 1915; *Under the Apple Trees*, 1916; *Field and Study*, 1919; *Accepting the Universe*, 1920; *Under the Maples*, 1921; *The Last Harvest*, 1922.

This pursuit of nature involved the "wistful Celt" with world-renowned figures such as President Theodore Roosevelt, with whom he camped in Yellowstone National Park (1903), and John Muir with whom he camped and explored sites such as the Grand Canyon and Yosemite National Park (1909). Two anecdotes about these two gentlemen stand out as illustrations of the extraordinary and the unbelievable found in the great outdoors by the inquisitive pioneer.

The setting of the first is a camp in the heart of Yellowstone National Park in 1903. President Theodore Roosevelt (who customarily addressed Burroughs as "Oom (Uncle) John") had stated his wish to go alone into the wilderness. His bodyguard, Major Pitcher, (this was before the days of the Secret Service) very naturally did not like the idea and wished to send an orderly with him. "No," said the President. "Put me up a lunch and let me go alone. I will surely come back." And back he surely came.

It was about five o'clock when Roosevelt strode briskly down the path to the camp from the east. It came out that he had tramped about eighteen miles through very rough terrain. The day before, he and Major Pitcher had located a band of several hundred elk on a broad, treeless hillside. His purpose was to find those elk again, creep up on them and eat his lunch under their very noses. And this he did, spending an hour or more within fifty yards of them. He came back looking as fresh as when he set out, and at night, sitting before a big campfire, he related his adventure. It is difficult to imagine that happening today when the President of the United States is under constant surveillance, day and night.

Some time later the President wrote warmly to Burroughs:

"My Dear Oom John,

"Every lover of outdoor life must feel a sense of affectionate obligation to you. Your writing appeals to all who care for the life of the woods and fields, whether their tasks keep them in the homely pleasant farm country or lead them into the wilderness. It is a good thing for our people that you have lived and surely no man can wish to have more said of him."

When John O'Birds (Burroughs) asked John O'Mountains (Muir) to name the most magnificent phenomenon he had ever witnessed, he replied without hesitation, "snow-banners." Muir's description of them follows:

"The peaks of the High Sierra, back of Yosemite Valley, on rare occasions would be decorated with snow-banners. Many of the starry snow-flowers, out of which these banners are made, fall

ABOVE: *Muir (John O'Mountains) stresses a point about Yosemite's geological structure as Burroughs (John O'Birds) listens with rapt attention while visiting in California in 1909.*

before they are ripe, while most of those that do attain perfect development as six-rayed crystals glint and chafe against one another in their fall through the frosty air, and are broken into dry fragments. . . .And whenever storm-winds find this prepared snow-dust in a loose condition on exposed slopes, where there is free upward sweep to leeward, it is tossed back into the sky, and borne onward from peak to peak in the form of banners. . . .

"The occurrence of well-formed banners is comparatively rare and I have seen only one display of this kind that seemed in every way perfect, when, while wintering in Yosemite Valley in 1873, a wild 'norther' swept its snow-laden summits.

"Indian Canyon, through which I climbed, was choked with snow that had been shot down in avalanches from the high cliffs on either side, rendering the ascent difficult; but inspired by the roaring storm, the tedious wallowing brought no fatigue, and in four hours I gained the top of the ridge above the valley, 8000 feet high. And there in bold relief, like a clear painting, appeared a most imposing scene. Innumerable peaks, black and sharp, rose grandly into the dark blue sky, their bases set in solid white, their sides streaked and splashed with snow, like the ocean rocks with foam; and from every summit, all free and unconfused, was streaming a beautiful silky silvery banner, from a half a mile to a mile in length, slender at the point of attachment, then widening gradually as it extended from the peak until it was about 1000 or 1500 feet in breadth, as near as I could estimate. The cluster of peaks called the "Crown of the Sierra," at the head of the Merced and Tuolumne Rivers—Mounts Dana, Gibbs, Conness, Lyell, Maclure, Ritter, with their nameless compeers—each had its own refulgent banner, waving with a clearly visible motion in the sunglow, and there was not a single cloud in the sky to mar their simple grandeur. . . .They are twenty miles away, but you would not wish them nearer, for every feature is distinct, and the whole glorious show is seen in its right proportions. . . .How grandly the banners wave as the wind is deflected against their sides, and how trimly each is attached to the very summit of its peak, like a streamer at a masthead; how smooth and silky they are in texture, and how finely their fading fringes are penciled on the azure sky."

These anecdotes illustrate the breadth of the experiences that Burroughs brought to the renowned Ford, Edison and Firestone camping trips. As he reflected in his diary at the time, "I'm more ready for an 'inning' rather than an outing." However, until shortly before his death in 1921, he was a most enjoyable, friendly and knowledgeable traveling companion.

Burroughs in his diary of the 1918 camping trip profiled his famous companions from an advantageous viewpoint. There had developed between them over a substantial period of time a bond of friendship; so he wrote from a position of close personal knowledge of these men, admittedly with a favorable bias.

"Our two chief characters presented many contrasts; Mr. Ford is more adaptive, more indifferent to places, than is Edison. His interest in the stream is in its potential water power. He races up and down its banks to see its fall, and where power could be developed. He is never tired of talking about how much power is going to waste everywhere, and says that if the streams were all harnessed, as they could easily be, farm labor everywhere, indoors and out, could be greatly lessened. He dilates on the benefit that would accrue to every country neighborhood if the water power that is going to waste in the valley streams were set to work in some useful industry, furnishing employment to the farmer and others in the winter season when their farms need comparatively little of their attention.

"Mr. Ford always thinks in terms of the greatest good to the greatest number. He aims to place all his inventions within the reach of the greatest mass of people. When he first went into the automobile business he associated himself with others in building a large expensive car, but very soon

ABOVE: *Burroughs, left, and his close friend John Muir pause for a moment's rest while exploring Yosemite National Park in California in 1909.*

saw that the need was for a car sufficiently low in price to place it within reach of the mass of the population. In building his tractor engine he has had the same end in view, so that now there is a machine on the market the price of which places it within the reach of nearly as many farmers as is the car. He does not forget the housewife either, and has plans for bringing power into every household that would greatly lighten the burden of the women folk. The old-fashioned grist-mills along the road with their huge overshot wheels were of never-failing interest to him.

"The behavior of Mr. Edison on such a trip is in marked contrast to that of Mr. Ford. Partly owing to his much greater age, but mainly, no doubt, to his more meditative and introspective cast of mind, he is far less active. When we paused for mid-day lunch, or to make camp at the end of the day, Mr. Edison would sit in his car reading, or curl up, boy fashion, under a tree and take a nap, while Mr. Ford would inspect the stream, or busy himself in getting wood for the fire.

"Mr. Ford is a runner and a high kicker, and frequently challenges some member of the party to race with him. He is also a persistent walker, and from every camp, both morning and evening, he sallied forth for a brisk half-hour walk. His cheerfulness and adaptability on all occasions, and his optimism in regard to all the great questions, are remarkable. His good-will and tolerance are as broad as the world. Notwithstanding his practical turn of the mind, and his mastery of the mechanical arts, and of the business methods, he is through and through an idealist.

"This combination of powers and qualities makes him a very interesting and, I may say, loveable personality. He is as tender as a woman, and much more tolerant. He looks like a poet, and conducts his life like a philosopher. No poet ever expressed himself through his work more completely than Mr. Ford has expressed himself through his car and his tractor engine. They typify him—not imposing, not complex, less expressive of power and mass than of simplicity, adaptability and universal service.

"Those who meet Mr. Ford are almost invariably drawn to him. He is a national figure, and the crowds that flock around the car in which he is riding, as we pause in the towns through which we pass, are not paying their homage merely to a successful car-builder, or business man, but to a beneficent great practical idealist, whose good-will and spirit of universal helpfulness they have all felt. He has not only brought pleasure and profit into their lives, but has illustrated and written large upon the pages of current history a new ideal of the business man—that of a man whose devotion to the public good has been a ruling passion, and whose wealth has inevitably flowed from the depth of his humanitarianism. He has taken the people into partnership with him and has eagerly shared with them the benefits that are the fruit of his great enterprise—a liberator, an emancipator, through channels that are so often used to enslave or destroy.

"In one respect, essentially the same thing may be said of Mr. Edison—he has become wealthy in spite of himself, through his great service to the whole civilized world. His first and leading thought has been, what can I do to make life easier and more enjoyable to my fellow man? He is a great chemist, a trenchant and original thinker on all of the great questions of life—a practical scientist, plus a meditative philosopher of profound insight. We all delight in his wise and witty sayings. He is a good camper-out and turns vagabond very easily. He can go with his hair uncombed and his clothes unbrushed as long as the best of us. He eats so little that I do not think he was tempted by the chicken roosts or turkey flocks along the way, nor by the corn fields and apple orchards, as some of us were. But there can be no doubt about his love for the open air and for wild nature. He can rough it week in and week out and be happy.

"Mr. Firestone belongs to an entirely different type—the clean, clearheaded, conscientious business type, always on his job, always ready for whatever comes, always at the service of those around him, a man devoted to his family and his friends, sound in his ideas, and generous of the wealth that has come to him as a manufacturer who has faithfully and honestly served his countrymen.

"When a man of letters like myself goes a-junketing with two such well-known men as Edison and Ford, he shines mainly by reflected light—he is in famous company. The public is eager to press the hand and hear the voice of these two men, but a writer of books excites interest only now and then. School teachers, editors, doctors, clergymen, lawyers, nature lovers, frequently gravitate to my side of the car, while the main crowd of working and business men goes to the other side."

PAN-PACIFIC

1915

1915
ITINERARY

Pan-Pacific Exposition In San Francisco, California

STOP 1   *Henry Ford and Thomas Edison arrived at the San Francisco Exposition in their private railroad cars and were greeted there by Harvey Firestone. Edison was honored with ceremonies at the fair grounds followed by a drive, hosted by Firestone, around San Francisco, California.*

STOP 2   *Entourage traveled by private railroad cars to Santa Rosa, California and visited with Luther Burbank.*

STOP 3   *Inspected San Quentin Prison on San Francisco Bay, followed by lunch there.*

STOP 4   *Private railroad cars taken to Riverside, California where the party viewed the motion picture-making process.*

STOP 5   *Toured by automobile to San Diego, California, stopping along the way to view the mission San Diego de Alcala.*

STOP 6   *Reached San Diego and participated in the Edison Day celebration at the Exposition. A getaway dinner was hosted by Firestone at the Fairmont Hotel in San Diego.*

STOP 7   *Ford returned to Dearborn, Michigan. Edison departed for West Orange, New Jersey with a stopover at the Grand Canyon, Arizona. Firestone remained in California on business.*

ABOVE: *This Pan-Pacific Exposition crowd is spellbound at the sight of, left to right, Harvey Firestone, Thomas Edison and Henry Ford at the rear of the automobile in San Francisco, California.*

1915

PAN-PACIFIC EXPOSITION

"In San Francisco, California"

The idea for camping trips had its germination in 1914 on a motor trip and picnic to the Florida Everglades by the Fords and Edisons and John Burroughs. The party included Henry Ford, his wife, Clara, and son, Edsel; Thomas Edison, his wife, Minerva ("Mina"), and sons Theodore and Charles.

When the Fords visited the Edisons in Fort Myers, Florida, in 1914, their hosts pointed out the advantages of a winter home there. So in December 1916, Henry and Clara Ford bought land and a house there for $20,000. To this they added, in June 1922, additional frontage for $13,500, which now gave them four acres next to the Edisons.

The camping idea took root in 1915 at the Pan-Pacific Exposition in San Francisco. The participants were Mr. and Mrs. Henry Ford; Mr. and Mrs. Thomas Edison; Edsel Ford; Harvey Firestone, Sr., and his wife, Idabelle; Billy Bee (Edison's secretary); Mr. and Mrs. Dutee Wilcox Flint (a Ford dealer); Flint's grandfather, Dutee Wilcox; Roy Bryant (Mrs. Ford's brother); and Grace Miller.

Thomas Edison and Henry Ford had traveled to the exposition in their private railroad cars for the Edison Day celebration in late October. An innovation at the fair was a banquet cooked entirely by electricity.

A reception committee greeted Edison at the railroad station as he descended from his Pullman car. After officiating at the ceremony that honored his brilliant achievements, he was taken for a drive around San Francisco by Harvey Firestone.

W. D'Arcy Ryan, who was in charge of illuminations at the Pan-Pacific Exposition, spent considerable time showing Edison and Ford around the fairgrounds, the tour culminating in a fantastic fireworks display that night.

After the fair, the group decided to take their private railroad cars up to Santa Rosa for a visit with Luther Burbank. Edison's botanical interest lay in growing plants that worked into some invention of his. Ford demonstrated a genuine interest in plants

ABOVE: *A very formal pose is struck for the San Francisco photographer by, left to right, Ford, Edison, Luther Burbank and Firestone at Burbank's residence in Santa Rosa, California.*

BELOW: *Firestone stands by as Edison enters the touring car before participating in Edison Day ceremonies at the l9l5 Pan-Pacific Exposition. Note Firestone's non-skid tires.*

and flowers, and Burbank's experiments with small garden peas—to develop a size that could be harvested by a machine—intrigued Ford because a machine, not men's hands, could do the task.

The trip by private railroad cars on to Los Angeles was interrupted by a brief stop for an inspection of the San Quentin Prison on the upper San Francisco Bay. Lunch was served at the prison and Ford—who was very active in prison work, and had made a standing offer to take parolees into his shops—was asked by the inmates for a speech. He graciously declined by just rising and bowing.

Both Edison and Ford wanted to get away from the commercialization and crowds, so at Firestone's behest they left the railroad cars at Riverside, California and motored at a leisurely pace to the scheduled Edison Day festivities at the San Diego Exposition.

As they descended from the train to board their automobiles, a battery of motion-picture cameras was there to greet them. They accepted an offer to stop by a motion-picture studio to see the making of a movie. Edison had pioneered movie-making when he set up his outdoor studio, the Black Mariah, in West Orange, New Jersey. He was prevailed upon to lay the cornerstone for a new building the studio was about to erect—but he was not prepared for the brass band escort to the site.

ABOVE: *Firestone and Ford strike up a conversation with a native Indian as they take a brief rest while en route to the 1915 San Diego Exposition. The mission San Diego de Alcala appears in the background.*

PAN-PACIFIC EXPOSITION *In San Francisco California*   29

ABOVE: *Ford, front seat, Edison, rear seat, and Firestone, standing, are in the midst of the admiring assemblage at the Edison Day celebration at the San Diego Exposition.*

BELOW: *The entourage stops to inspect the Mission San Diego de Alcala, located six miles north of San Diego, California.*

Eventually they reached San Diego, arriving in the afternoon for Edison Day. The crowds were enormous as Edison gave a reception for the children at the exposition grounds, with each child tossing a bunch of flowers as the procession passed, until Edison stood waist deep in their fragrance.

The inclusion of farm tractors at this exposition pleased Henry Ford because he was starting to produce the Fordson tractors, which were being shipped to England to further the war effort. There was no unanimity on the point because Edison naturally favored the electric motor and Ford the gasoline engine.

One theme of the trip that recurred on several future camping trips was the potiential of waterpower for reducing manufacturing costs and enhancing mankind's prosperity. Harvey Firestone later revealed that Ford's extensive hydroelectric development dated from this California trip. Edison concurred that waterpower was the way to go.

Firestone hosted a getaway dinner at the Fairmont Hotel with a fine Hawaiian band and dancers. A good time was enjoyed by all—in fact, so good that Henry Ford hired the whole band and their families and returned with them to Detroit, where they worked and played for him.

The warm camaraderie that prevailed induced Edison to propose a camping trip for the next year for the threesome—Ford, Firestone and himself—as he departed for home by way of the Grand Canyon. Firestone remained in California for a while to look after his tire business.

So began a unique relationship that would prevail for a decade. It was time to prepare for the open road and the pleasure of roughing it.

LABORATORY

1916

PROVINCE OF QUEBEC

Malone · Chateaugay Lakes · Chazy

Plattsburg

Paul Smiths · Keeseville
Saranac Lake · Lake Placid · Ausable Forks
Essex
Elizabethtown
West Port

ADIRONDACK MOUNTAINS

Long Lake · Tahawus · Schroon River

Blue Mountain Lake

Indian Lake

LAKE CHAMPLAIN

Winooski
Burlington
Shelburne

Middlebury

Rutland

Wallingford

LAKE GEORGE

Lake George

Corinth

Saratoga Springs

Schenectady

Albany

CATSKILLS

Catskill

Phoenicia

Ellenville · Highland · PoughKeepsie

Newburgh

NEW YORK STATE

VERMONT

East Dorset
Manchester
Arlington
Bennington

Pittsfeild

Lenox

Great Barrington

MASS

Amenia · Hartford

CONN

HUDSON RIVER

NEW JERSEY

Pompton

Paterson

Orange

NewHaven
Bridgeport

LONG ISLAND SOUND

Long Island

1916
ITINERARY

In Nature's Laboratory, the Adirondacks and Green Mountains of New England

AUGUST 28   *Left Orange, New Jersey, at 9:50 a.m., stopped eight miles from Ellenville, New York, to camp after having traveled the Pompton Turnpike through the Catskills and Newfoundland. Distance: 82.8 miles.*

AUGUST 29   *Left at 9:50 a.m. passing through Ellenville, Phoenicia, Arkville and Fleischmanns, New York, arriving at John Burroughs's at 5 p.m. and then camping in the orchard at Woodchuck Lodge, Roxbury. Distance: 97 miles.*

AUGUST 30   *Left Roxbury, at 1:30 p.m. driving through the Catskills to Albany, arriving at 8:30 p.m. Distance: 95 miles.*

AUGUST 31   *Left Albany at 12:15 p.m. A. C. Miller joined the camping party, and J. G. Robertson, H. L. Adams and H. W. Smith were guests for lunch about fifteen miles from Albany. Passed through Cohoes and Saratoga Springs and camped in Pine Woods, one mile from Corinth, New York. Distance: 55 miles.*

SEPTEMBER 1 *Left the Pine Woods camp at 10:30 a.m., passing through Lake George. Set up camp on the Babcock place at Indian Lake, New York, at 6:30 p.m. Distance: 74 miles.*

SEPTEMBER 2 *Left the Babcock camp at 10:45 a.m., passing through Blue Mountain Lake, Tahawus and Schroon River; pitched camp on the Sharow farm three miles from Elizabethtown, New York. Distance: 95 miles.*

SEPTEMBER 3 *Left the Sharow camp at 11:10 a.m., Miller parting from the group at Westport. Through Essex, Keeseville, Ausable Chasm, and on to Ausable Forks, where camp was pitched on a bend of the Ausable River, two miles from Ausable Forks. Distance: 64 miles.*

SEPTEMBER 4 *Started at 10:45 a.m., drove through Lake Placid, Saranac Lake, Paul Smiths, and camped eighteen miles from Malone, New York. Distance: 73 miles.*

SEPTEMBER 5 *Left camp at 9 a.m., passing through Malone and Moores; arrived at Plattsburgh, New York, at 3 p.m. Camped on the Behan farm, one mile from Plattsburgh. Distance: 82 miles.*

SEPTEMBER 6 *After seeing the Plattsburgh Fair, left with John Myers as a guest at 12:15 p.m. to ferry from Chazy Landing past LaMotte, Grand Isle and North Hero, Vermont, and pitched camp at Winooski, a suburb of Burlington. Distance: 69 miles.*

SEPTEMBER 7 *Myers left the party at 10 a.m. and the group continued through Burlington, Shelburne, Middlebury, Rutland, Wallingford, East Dorset, Manchester, and camped near Arlington. The camp was dubbed Camp Bronson. Distance: 114 miles.*

SEPTEMBER 8 *Left Camp Bronson at 9 a.m., passing through Bennington, Vermont; Pittsfield (Professor DeLoach left the group here); Lenox, Great Barrington and Sheffield, Massachusetts; Lakeville, Connecticut; Armenia, New York and made the six o'clock ferry at Poughkeepsie, then camped on Reverend Allen's place four miles from Highland at 6:45 p.m. Distance: 143.5 miles.*

SEPTEMBER 9 *John Burroughs left, motoring to his home, Slabsides, with his son, Julian. The rest left at 9:30 a.m., going through Newburgh, Harriman, Tuxedo and Suffern, New York; Pompton and Montclair, New Jersey, before arriving in Orange at 3 p.m. Distance: 73 miles. Total number of miles traveled: 1,117.3.*

ABOVE: *Edison and Firestone at Edison's laboratories in West Orange, New Jersey, with the vehicles "at the ready" for the start of the 1916 camping trip.*

1916

IN NATURE'S LABORATORY

"The Adirondacks and Green Mountains of New England"

After much correspondence it was agreed that Harvey Firestone should meet Thomas Edison at West Orange, New Jersey, to inaugurate the 1916 trip. The plan was to motor to New York to meet Burroughs; Ford had indicated he would join them at some point along the journey. Firestone, as commissary chief, took along plenty of provisions and a good cook. Edison provided the equipment, with his special pride being a storage battery hookup for lighting the camp and tents for this camp and future camps.

Rain fell heavily on the morning of August 28, 1916, then tapered off as Edison and Firestone, accompanied by Professor R. J. H. DeLoach, a director of the Armour Company and a close friend of Burroughs and Harvey Firestone, Jr., left West Orange for their meeting with Burroughs at Roxbury, New York. As the photo at the top of the next page shows, three other Firestone executives also were with the party at the outset. Such "floating" personnel would often join the troupe at intermittent times on the various trips. After motoring on the Pompton Turnpike, through the Catskills and Newfoundland, they made camp by a creek eight miles from Ellenville, New York.

Just after they had settled in, a farmer rushed up to find out what they were doing there and to say that whatever it was, they should move on. At this juncture Firestone, with great assurance, mentioned that one of the group was Thomas Edison. But that didn't faze the farmer, and his tirade included the comment that "tramps and gypsies" were not welcome, even if one of them was named Edison! Of course, this was settled by giving him what he wanted in the first place—the omnipotent five-dollar bill.

August 29 dawned wet and cold. A 9:50 a.m. getaway time saw the party move through Ellenville, Phoenicia, Arkville and Fleischmanns, New York,. before arriving at 5 p.m. at John Burroughs's Woodchuck Lodge at Roxbury, and making camp in his orchard. Burroughs's journal entry in August 1916 recorded the event:

"August 29 came Edison and his party to take me with them on a motor-trip. They camped in my orchard, an unwonted sight—

ABOVE: *The camping participants line up outside the Edison laboratories, West Orange, New Jersey. Left to right: H. L. Adams, purchasing department, Firestone Corporation; J. G. Robertson, treasurer, Firestone Corporation; Edison; Harvey Firestone, Sr.; A. C. Miller, vice-president and director, Firestone Corporation; and Harvey Firestone, Jr.*

BELOW: *Movie men and press photographers await the appearance of the famous travelers at the Edison laboratories on August 26, 1916.*

a camper's extemporized village under my old apple trees—4 tents, a large dining-tent, and at night electric lights. And the man, Edison, the center around which it all revolved."

Burroughs, whose interests lay in his surroundings of trees, birds and wildlife, much removed from the frenetic business world, felt little inclined to join up with the campers. The cold weather and advanced age combined to conspire against his acceptance of their invitation. Edison had looked forward to Burroughs's inspiring him with his botanical knowledge and skill, so disappointment prevailed with the octogenarian's reluctance.

That evening as they sat around the dining table in the orchard, under the pale-green canopy lighted by electric lights, eating the elaborate dinner which the English chef, Endicott, had prepared, the modern Merlin sat at the head of the table dining on toast and hot milk, saying of his frugal fare, "This suits me best—but I could live for days just on the news of Rumania joining the Allies." The talk between Edison and Burroughs around the campfire, and the sight of their white heads in the firelight, there under the old apple trees, were memorable. Their chat covered a wide range—dietetics, recent discoveries in chemistry and physics, the latest developments of the war, boyhood reminiscences, primitive man—the last suggested by a recognition of what awakens in everyone at the sight of a fire in the open.

The good dinner, and the warm bond that developed between the campers and negated the chill of the night air, worked their magic: Burroughs suddenly announced that he would be ready to go in the morning. Camaraderie had prevailed.

The night was very cold, but Edison would not let them yield to temptation even a little, refusing to let them bring their cots onto the

veranda and declaring they must not begin by coddling themselves. Edison simply basked in "Nature's primal sanities." Laboratories and other work for that busy brain ceased to exist.

August 30 dawned with clearing weather, camp was struck and the caravan left at 1:30 p.m. bound for the Catskills and Albany, New York. After arriving in Albany at 8:30 p.m., Harvey Firestone telephoned Henry Ford, who said he would be along in two or three days and that they would meet at the Hotel Champlain in Plattsburgh, New York.

The following day at noontime, with a stop fifteen miles from Albany and lunch with some Firestone executives, another humorous incident occurred. It seems that the group found an ideal spot for their repast at an abandoned, half-ruined farmhouse. Moments after the table was set in the driveway, a couple of women drove up and waxed indignant. Firestone asked if they objected to the lunch activity and was met with a resounding "Yes!" To the next question, "Do you own the property?" came the rebuttal, "No, but it belongs to our grandmother." No response was forthcoming to an offer to pay damages, and off the women drove. Hardly had they left when a large hay wagon turned into the driveway. Edison yelled to the driver to wait a short while. The driver responded, "I dunno, this load is pretty heavy." "Will you wait for two dollars?" "Yes." Then he took the money, and with a grin promptly drove around the table barrier!

During the afternoon, motoring resumed through the towns of Cohoes and Saratoga Springs until camp was made in Pine Woods, one mile from Corinth, New York.

September arrived while the campers were breaking camp and preparing to leave at 10:30 a.m. They drove a distance of seventy-

ABOVE: *Edison and Firestone dutifully give time to press photographers at Edison's laboratories, West Orange, New Jersey.*

BELOW: *Left to right, Burroughs, Firestone, Dr. Clara Barrus Burroughs's assistant, and Edison lunch in the orchard at Woodchuck Lodge as Burroughs is being prevailed upon to join in the camping trip.*

ABOVE: *A close-up of Dr. Clara Barrus, naturalist, physician, friend and secretary to Burroughs, after lunch in the orchard with, left to right, Firestone, Edison and Burroughs.*

RIGTH: *Harvey Firestone and John Burroughs relax on the rustic porch of Woodchuck Lodge, in Roxbury, New York.*

BELOW: *"Lunch on Grandmother's lawn," so named for the claim by two women passing by that the property was owned by their grandmother. Left to right: H. W. Smith, secretary to Firestone, H. L. Adams, J. G. Robertson, A. C. Miller (standing), Burroughs, Edison, and the Firestones.*

four miles through to Lake George and on to the Babcock farm at Indian Lake, where camp was set up at 6:30 p.m.

John Burroughs would later pen an account of this camp in which he described his own and Edison's geological and camping experiences. He reminisced that at the Indian Lake camp Edison at one time had his hands full of disintegrated granite and pointed out to Burroughs the different mineral elements it contained and their various uses. The feldspar was a source of the potash which he hoped to obtain on a scale that would make the United States independent of the Germans for this material. Edison foresaw a foundry perfected to extract potash on a commercial scale from granite rocks, of which the Adirondacks would afford an inexhaustible supply. Unfortunately, that venture in New Jersey later nearly bankrupted him when competition appeared from Michigan's Upper Peninsula mineral fields.

Burroughs also commented on the great pleasure it was to see Edison relax and turn vagabond so easily, sleeping in his clothes, curling up at lunchtime on a blanket under a tree and dropping off to sleep like a baby, getting up to replenish the campfire at daybreak or

before, making his toilet at the creek or wayside pool, and more than that, to see him practice what he preached about avoiding excessive eating, at each meal taking only a little toast and a cup of hot milk.

"The luxuries of our 'Waldorf-Astoria' on wheels that followed us everywhere had little attraction for Mr. Edison," Burroughs said. "One cold nite he hit on a new way of folding his blankets; he made them interlock so-and-so, then got into them, made one revolution and the thing was done."

September 2 turned out to be another routine day on the road, with a start of 10:45 a.m. after camp was struck and the gear packed

ABOVE: *Burroughs and Edison take a moment to enjoy some reading material on the porch of "Grandmother's house," near Albany, following the noontime lunch break on August 31.*

ABOVE: *A mineralogy study at the Indian Lake camp undertaken by experts Burroughs and Edison.*

RIGHT: *The camp in Pine Woods, one mile from Corinth, New York, on August 31. At the left is the camp cook, H. E. Endicott. Seated are A. C. Miller, Professor R. J. H. DeLoach (Armour Company), Firestone, Edison and Burroughs.*

ABOVE: *A quiet moment is shared after the tents are set up and the campfire srtarted at the camp on Sharow's farm, three miles from Elizabethtown, New York.*

LEFT: *The camping caravan stops to commune with Mother Nature while traveling through the Catskills toward Albany, New York. The lead automobile contains George Williams, driver, and Edison, in the front seat, with Burroughs, A. C. Miller and Firestone occupying the rear seat.*

LEFT: *The camping group is almost ready to depart at the breaking of the Indian Lake camp on September 2, 1916.*

ABOVE: *The hotel at Blue Mountain Lake, reported to be the first building in the world equipped with electric lights by Edison.*

ABOVE: *"The Triumvirate" enjoys a moment of quiet reflection at the Ausable River camp. Left to right: Burroughs, Edison and Firestone.*

BELOW: *A great spot to get away from the admiring crowds of the towns and cities. Fred Ott is seated in the tent while Burroughs, Firestone and Edison are seated by the Ausable River.*

away. They traveled to Blue Mountain Lake to view an interesting historical building—the hotel which was the first building in the world to be equipped with electric lights. Long Lake was then visited, also Tahawus and Schroon River, and finally camp was made on the Sharow farm about three miles from Elizabethtown, New York. The distance from Camp Babcock to Camp Sharow was ninety-five miles.

After breaking camp the following day, September 3, they started at 11:10 a.m. toward Westport, New York, where a guest, A. C. Miller, a Firestone director, left the group. Then the entourage followed the trail through Essex, Keeseville, Ausable Chasm and on to Ausable Forks, where camp was made on a bend of the Ausable River, just two miles from the fork. This area was a highlight of the excursion, according to Burroughs: "I had never before seen the Adirondacks under such favourable conditions; seen as we saw them, lined up in great procession, they are impressive. They take the conceit out of my native Catskills. Their vast geologic age awesome; holding their heads so high after a hundred or more million of years; and their magnitude and primordial look all stir the imagination. In them we behold the source of much of the land out of which You and I come."

Harvey Firestone later related a humorous adventure that occurred at this Ausable camp. Edison planned the trip and made rules for it, one of them being that no one should shave. This night turned cold and it was decided that Burroughs had better not sleep out, so Firestone drove him over to a hotel in Ausable Forks, leaving Edison

ABOVE: *The dining area of the camp on the curve of the Ausable River, New York. The camp cook, H. E. Endicott, is on the left. Relaxing are Harvey Firestone, Jr., Burroughs, Harvey Firestone, Sr., and Edison.*

LEFT: *A stop for lunch along the country road while en route to Elizabethtown, New York. Edison is seated in the automobile. Seated by the roadside are Firestone, A. C. Miller, Burroughs and DeLoach. Standing are Mr. Lee and H. C. Endicott.*

and Harvey Firestone, Jr., in camp.

"When I saw the hotel bedroom and bath, I could stand the strain no longer and I struck. Not only did I have a shave and a bath, but I also spent the night comfortably in bed. I did not know what was going to happen when I reached the camp in the morning with Mr. Burroughs and saw Mr. Edison and Harvey Firestone, Jr., alone at breakfast. Mr. Edison saw at once that I had shaved. He did not so much mind having me out all night, but he did object to the rules-breaking shave."

Edison, with a laugh, commented that Firestone was a "tenderfoot" and would soon be dressing up like a "dude." Good nature prevailed.

September 4 saw a start at a respectable 10:45 a.m. after they had breakfasted, taken care of personal needs and broken camp. A leisurely drive took them through the beautiful fall countryside bedecked with the jewels that were Lake Placid, Saranac Lake and the quaint town of Paul Smiths. Camp was set up on a farm eighteen miles from Malone, New York. A rather early departure from camp was accomplished at 9 a.m. on the morning of September 5 with an immediate destination of Malone, which turned out to be the northernmost point of this camping trip. The following newspaper account aptly

BELOW: *A serene scene around the campfire as the day's activity gives way to silent reflection. The relaxed campers are, left to right, Firestone, Mr. Sharow (farm owner), Burroughs, Edison and A. C. Miller.*

ABOVE: *At the entrance to the Flanagan Hotel in Malone, New York, the campers are met by the hotel owner, Jack Flanagan. Left to right: Firestone, Burroughs, Edison and Jack Flanagan. In early September in upper New York State heavy outer garments were in order to combat the damp chill of the air.*

relates the condition and activities of the campers as they "hit town":

"Malone was host, briefly, to three of the world's great in science and industry when Thomas A. Edison, John Burroughs, the naturalist, and Harvey S. Firestone, the pioneer tire-maker, passed through here on September 5, 1916, on an automobile jaunt which was considered quite an intrepid undertaking what with hard-starting motors and frequent blowouts.

"These distinguished argonauts whirled into town, trailed by a dust cloud. They rode a high-roofed Simplex touring car while behind them followed Mr. Firestone's son in a Ford runabout with a White truck bringing up the rear. The truck carried camping equipment, for the three friends were roughing it on the trip, living in the open and disdaining the comfort of hotels. They had tented the previous nite near Chasm Falls where the world's greatest inventor, now 69 years old, had chopped wood and helped cook breakfast.

"It was natural that this cavalcade of celebrated personages should be greeted by Jack Flanagan of the Flanagan Hotel for Mr. Flanagan is famed as a host wherever the name of Malone is known.

They were induced to pose for a photograph at the hotel entrance—a comparatively shabby appearing trio with Chasm Falls mud still clinging to their shoes. All three were roughly dressed for their outdoor life. The only incongruous note in this back-to-nature junket was the presence of Mr. Firestone's sober-faced English butler, Endicott, who had once been Chef to the Lord of Devonshire. But Mr. Firestone hastened to explain that the admirable Endicott did only his share of the chores.

"Mr. Edison remarked pridefully that he had rigged up a lighting system for the travelers' tent, using an Edison battery. By this light the voyagers sat late into the evening before a camp-fire listening to the wildlife stories of the white-bearded Mr. Burroughs. They were enroute to Plattsburgh where they would be joined by Henry Ford, described as 'an automaker and a pacifist.' Mr. Firestone didn't hesitate to point out that the vehicles in his party were all well-shod with Firestone tires. He regarded the extra tires as unnecessary baggage.

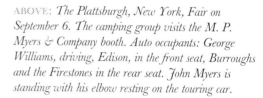

ABOVE: *The Plattsburgh, New York, Fair on September 6. The camping group visits the M. P. Myers & Company booth. Auto occupants: George Williams, driving, Edison, in the front seat, Burroughs and the Firestones in the rear seat. John Myers is standing with his elbow resting on the touring car.*

BELOW LEFT: *The camp at Winooski, near Burlington, Vermont. Edison occupies his regular seat in the parked auto as H. E. Endicott peers into the tent. Also posing for the cameraman are, left to right, DeLoach, Harvey Firestone, Sr., and Harvey Jr., flanking Burroughs*

BELOW: *Lunchtime is a welcome break as the travelers approach Rutland, Vermont. Enjoying the repast are, left to right, DeLoach, Firestone, Edison and Burroughs.*

ABOVE: *A quiet hour at Camp Bronson, near Arlington, Vermont, offers Burroughs and Firestone an opportunity to catch up on some reading.*

BELOW: *The camping gear has dried out, from the early morning dew, and the ever reliable crew is packing up for the trip to the next campsite. With this activity Camp Bronson is secured.*

'With Firestone tires we'll never have a blowout,' he grinned."

After stopping for lunch outside Malone, the camping party proceeded through Moores and arrived at Plattsburgh at approximately three in the afternoon. Edison, as prearranged with Henry Ford, stopped in town for word of the automaker's plans to accompany them. The following telegram, sent by Ernest G. Liebold, Ford's business secretary, tells the story:

Detroit–Sept. 4, 1916
Thomas Edison
Lake Champlain Hotel
Plattsburgh, N.Y.

Regret very much to inform you that Mr. Ford has finally decided to leave for coast tomorrow morning as Mr. Perry and family must return to England end of this month and he therefore would not have time to join you and make western trip as well. However he expects to arrange for a real camping vacation sometime during the coming winter when he hopes to make up for the disappointment occasioned through his inability to go this time.

E. G. LIEBOLD

Despite Ford's intentions, the next year, 1917, being a war year, posed many scheduling problems for the group, so it proved to be 1918 before this stellar combination of personalities could camp together.

The group's disappointment at Ford's no-show did not dampen

the camper's spirits for long as Edison steered them to a campsite one mile from town, on the Behan farm. The weather remained mild and overcast as supper was taken and the ever-present campfire was again the setting for enjoyment, contentment and the bonding of sincere relationships.

September 6 provided an opportunity to attend a fair in Plattsburgh during the forenoon. John Myers, a Firestone dealer, had been a camping guest the night before and now served as host, pointing out the highlights of the fair, including his motor dealership exhibit. Getaway time was 12:15 p.m., and after a short jaunt to Chazy Landing, with time out for a lunch break, the vehicles were loaded aboard the ferry for an enjoyable voyage across Lake Champlain, sailing past LaMotte, Grand Isle and North Hero with a landing in Vermont, where camp was pitched at Winooski, a suburb

ABOVE: *This was horse riding time for Reverend Allen's daughters at the camp near Highland, New York. Left to right: Firestone, Reverend Allen's daughters, the Reverend and Edison.*

RIGHT: *The noonday siesta after lunch while en route to the final destination of West Orange, New Jersey, September 9. Firestone relaxes in a camp chair as Edison snoozes beneath the tree.*

of Burlington.

The following morning Myers departed for Plattsburgh, New York, while the caravan entered the open road at 10 a.m., passing through Burlington, Shelburne and Middlebury before stopping for lunch near Rutland.

Harvey Firestone privately published a book for his close friends about this 1916 camping trip entitled "In Nature's Laboratory." Firestone describes this lunchtime in the following verse:

> Down in the Vermont country
> Where the air is bracing
> and the spirits bound,
> In a field by the roadside
> With a flowered carpet found,
> Adding zest to zealous appetites
> A tonic e'en
> in between bites!

BELOW: *John Burroughs left the camping party at Reverend Allen's place near Highland, New York. A fond farewell is extended by Firestone and Edison while Burroughs's son, Julian, stands next to the auto. Reverend Allen is at right.*

Following this repast it was on to Wallingford, East Dorset, Manchester, with a camp set up near Arlington. This camp, being on the Bronson farm, was appropriately named Camp Bronson.

An early rise enabled a 9 a.m. getaway from camp on September 8, then a short jaunt through Bennington to Pittsfield, Massachusetts, where a fond farewell was accorded Professor R. J. H. DeLoach upon his departure. The afternoon segment consisted in traveling through Lenox, where lunch and a siesta revitalized the explorers; Great Barrington; Sheffield; Lakeville, Connecticut; and Armenia,

New York, with an appointed time of precisely 6 p.m. for a rendezvous with the ferry at Poughkeepsie that carried all their complement across the Hudson River. Forty-five minutes later, camp was set up on the farm of Reverend Allen, just four miles from Highland, New York. The mileage this day—143.5 miles—was the greatest for any of the camping days.

John Burroughs's son, Julian, arrived on the morning of September 9 to escort his father back to the family home, Slabsides, in West Park, New York. Heartfelt farewells were exchanged between this loveable octogenarian and the other distinguished campers.

After passing a few pleasant moments with the Reverend Allen and his two comely daughters, they broke up this final camp. The open road beckoned one final time, at 9:30 a.m., for the trip through Newburgh, Harriman and Tuxedo, New York. A midday lunch break was taken along a country road on this leg of the journey to Orange, New Jersey, followed by the customary siesta, which was captured by Firestone's verse:

ABOVE: *Reverend Allen and Burroughs could be discussing "God's creation of Nature" while the crew breaks camp at Reverend Allen's place near Highland, New York.*

> We've fasted and feasted and scanned the news,
> The spot's ideal for a snooze,
> While the bees drone out a lullaby
> And care perfects its alibi!

The final run was through Suffern, New York and Pompton and Montclair, New Jersey, with a 3 p.m. arrival at Orange. The distance attained this day was 73 miles. The highly successful and enjoyable 1916 camping trip covered 1,117.3 miles in thirteen days.

BELOW: *A lunch break with the camp workers while en route back to Orange, New Jersey. Seated, Firestone and Edison, standing, Mr. Johns, Mr. Lee, H. E. Endicott, George Williams and Frederick Ott.*

1918

1918

ITINERARY

The Vacation Days of 1918 in the Land of Dixie

AUGUST 16-17 *Thomas Edison, John Burroughs and Professor R. J. H. DeLoach motored from Orange, New Jersey, to Pittsburgh, Pennsylvania, where they were joined by Commissioner Edward N. Hurley. Henry Ford, Harvey Firestone, Sr. and Jr., met at the Firestone homestead in Columbiana, Ohio, then proceeded to Pittsburgh.*

AUGUST 18 *Assembled party left Pittsburgh Sunday afternoon, going through Greensburg, Pennsylvania, and made first camp (Camp Hurley) two miles east of Greensburg.*

AUGUST 19 *Broke camp at 11 a.m., as Commissioner Hurley had to leave for Washington, D.C.; passed through Connellsville, Pennsylvania, on the way to Summit Mountain and stopped at the Summit Hotel in Uniontown.*

AUGUST 20 *After an early start, stopped at Keysers Ridge, Maryland, for mail, on through Oakland to Leadmine, West Virginia, camped at Horse Shoe Run.*

AUGUST 21 *Drove to Elkins, West Virginia, on through Beverly to Cheat Mountain, spent the night there at Camp Cheat.*

AUGUST 22 *Left Camp Cheat, at 10 a.m., enjoyed cradling and bundling contest near Bartow and camped at Bolar Springs, Virginia.*

AUGUST 23 *Left Bolar Springs, at 9 a.m., visited phosphate plant en route to Hot Springs, and on through White Sulphur Springs, West Virginia to Camp Tuckahoe.*

AUGUST 24 *Broke camp early, passed through Sweet Springs, West Virginia, lunched at Gap Mills, on through Narrows, Virginia, and camped at Wolf Creek.*

AUGUST 25 *Left Wolf Creek, passed through Oakvale, Princeton, and Bluefield, West Virginia, then made camp at Tazewell, Virginia.*

AUGUST 26 *Left Camp Tazewell, passed through Lebanon, Hansonville and Abingdon and lunched at a hotel in Bristol, Virginia-Tennessee, then continued on through Bluff City, Elizabethton and Johnson City, Tennessee, and made camp (Camp Robert E. Lee) just beyond Jonesborough, Tennessee.*

AUGUST 27 *Broke camp early, passed through Greenville and Newport, Tennessee, before arriving at Hot Springs, North Carolina, where they visited a German prisoner of war camp. Trip resumed to Mars Hill, on through Weaverville, and the campers arrived in Asheville, North Carolina, at 8:30 p.m., where they spent the night at the Grove Park Inn.*

AUGUST 28 *Burroughs, accompanied by Professor DeLoach, left by train for New York State; the camping equipment was sent home and the travelers proceeded to end the vacation by motoring. Drove through Marion before retiring at the Hotel Huffy in Hickory, North Carolina.*

AUGUST 29 *Left Hickory, passed through Statesville and Mocksville and lunched at the Forsythe Country Club in Winston-Salem, North Carolina. Motored to the Broad Street Hotel in Martinsville, Virginia, where they secured lodgings.*

AUGUST 30 *An early start was made for Roanoke, Virginia, then on to Natural Bridge for sight-seeing and dinner. They arrived that evening at the Castle Inn in Lexington, Virginia.*

AUGUST 31 *After a 7 a.m. breakfast, they motored to Staunton for lunch, then proceeded through Winchester before reaching Hagerstown, Maryland and the Hotel Hamilton. Nineteen tolls were paid between Staunton and Winchester.*

SEPTEMBER 1 *The vacation trip ended at noon as the travelers motored a few miles outside Hagerstown, Maryland, where they bade each other farewell.*

ABOVE: *The campers assemble at the Firestone Corporation branch in Pittsburgh, Pennsylvania before the start of the 1918 camping trip. Left to right: Edward N. Hurley, John Burroughs, Thomas Edison, Henry Ford, Harvey Firestone and Professor R. J. H. DeLoach.*

1918

THE VACATION DAYS OF 1918

"In The Land of Dixie"

A trip had been planned for 1917, but the coming war consumed too much of the industrialists' time for them to adequately provide for a camping excursion. By the time 1918 rolled around, camping fever had struck again and plans were formulated to get away for a much-needed rest to recharge their batteries. This trip through the Smoky Mountains and the Shenandoah Valley contained all the ingredients for success and was characterized by Harvey Firestone as "the best one we ever had."

Henry Ford traveled to the Firestone homestead in Columbiana, Ohio, on August 16, 1918, to join Harvey Firestone, Sr., and Harvey Firestone, Jr. The next day the ladies' aid society of the Grace Reformed Church gave a dinner for Firestone's superintendents and foremen, with Henry Ford as their guest of honor.

On Sunday morning, August 18, the threesome left the farm at 10 a.m. to motor to the William Penn Hotel in Pittsburgh, Pennsylvania, where they arrived at 2:30 p.m. At this time Thomas Edison, John Burroughs, Edward N. Hurley (commissioner of the U.S. Shipping Board) and Professor R. J. H. DeLoach were lunching at the home of Mr. Hitchcock (Edison's brother-in-law).

John Burroughs later humorously described his drive to Pittsburgh:

"The preliminary drive with Edison and DeLoach from Orange, New Jersey, to Pittsburgh, Pennsylvania, nearly four hundred miles in two days, was, for me, too big a dose at the outset. In our furious speed the car fairly kicked up its heels at times and we were unseated all too often. It was not easy to unseat Mr. Edison beside the chauffeur—there is a good deal of him to unseat, and he is cushiony and adjustable, and always carries his own shock absorbers with him. My own equipment of that sort disappeared long ago."

Edison needed this shaking up as an antidote to his concentrated life of experimentation in his laboratory. Ford, Firestone and DeLoach brought with them the keen edge of youth, blunted

ABOVE: *Ford pauses beside his Model T Ford truck, which sprang to life under his magical touch.*

only here and there, and Burroughs was at a distinct disadvantage in trying to keep up with them.

The trio had found Pennsylvania to be an impressive state, so vast, so diversified, so forest clad; the huge unbroken Allegheny ranges with their deep valleys cutting across from north to south, the world of fine farms and rural homesteads in the western half and the great mining and manufacturing interests; the source of noble rivers and the storehouse of some of nature's most useful gifts to mankind.

The great Lincoln Highway follows the line of least resistance, but it has some formidable obstacles to surmount. En route they passed many army trucks traveling east in procession, loaded with soldiers, equipment, weapons and materiel destined for the great seaports and the impending doom of the kaiser.

Pittsburgh, at this time, was a city that sat with its feet in brimstone and fire and its head in the sweet country air of the hilltops. Burroughs painted the following picture: "It might as well be the devil's laboratory. Out of such blackening and blasting fumes comes our civilization. That weapons of war and destructiveness should come out of such pits and abysses of hell-fire seems fit and natural, but much more comes out of them—much that suggests the pond lily rising out of the black slime and muck of the lake's bottom."

All the party members converged on the Firestone branch, where they awaited the belated arrival of a heavily laden Ford truck being piloted by a R.V. Kline. He was late because his brakes had worn out and he had had to back down hills. Pictures were taken (Harvey Firestone always had a photographer present) and interviews given to newspaper reporters. Then came the chore of transferring part of Kline's heavy load from the Ford to a ton-and-a-half White truck. Then the entourage, which consisted of six vehicles (two of them big autos and two of them flivvers) with the two trucks, and a seven-man crew, was ready to venture out of Pittsburgh on the way to Greensburg, Pennsylvania, being guided to the outskirts by

Mr. and Mrs. Hitchcock.

The first camp was set up about a half mile off the roadway in a beautiful oak grove near a well on the farm of H. A. Miller. Tents were laid out on a gentle eminence, well carpeted with grass, with wood and water in abundance. The cooks prepared a delicious supper, which was enjoyed around a big campfire where the campers lingered to swap stories (many unreportable!) until midnight. The pressures of the war dictated that this would be the only night that Commissioner Hurley would be in camp, for he left the next day.

Much of the fireside talk before they turned in gave insight into the many things that were uppermost in their minds. The ship question (World War I) was the question of the hour, and the perfect authority was at hand, Hurley, who provided comfort and assurance with his first-hand knowledge. It was quite in character for Ford to seem more lenient toward the enemy than were the rest, though he was no less determined to win the war. "We must win," he said, "and to do it we shall have to use up a lot of our resources. It is all waste, but it seems necessary, and we are ready to pay the price." At the beginning of the war he was a declared pacifist and let his heart run away with his head. He was never a seeker of notoriety, as some charged, but a seeker of the world's good. His unfortunate Peace Ship expedition did more credit to his big heart than to his judgment. But as the war went on, he became more convinced that the Allies' cause was a righteous one and threw himself heart and soul into the fray.

The night was chilly, and folding cots being a poor conserver of bodily warmth, it took the campers quite a while, once they finally decided to retire, to get the hang of them and equip themselves with plenty of blankets to ward off the chill. Sleep tarried but briefly with Burroughs, who arose about three or four in the morning to replenish the fire, and in a camp chair beside it indulged in the "long, long thoughts" which belong to age much more than to youth. Youth was soundly and audibly sleeping in the tents, with no thoughts at all.

RIGHT: *Ford proves to have a sharp eye and a steady hand while shooting "mark" at the camp in Pennsylvania.*

Everyone arose around 8 a.m. for breakfast, August 19, and a test of marksmanship. Greensburg's mayor and local newspapermen paid the camp a visit during the morning hours, while Commissioner Hurley bade farewell to the campers as he departed for Washington, D.C. Camp was struck at 11 a.m. for the move on to Greensburg, where gas and oil and a duster for Burroughs were purchased; then they continued toward Connellsville.

Here the Packard car, driven by Harvey Firestone, Jr., in which Ford and Harvey senior were riding, was disabled when the fan iron broke and punctured the radiator. Ford's mechanical genius, the worn parts and a few tools from the automobile toolbox were enough to get the car to a repair garage at Connellsville. Within ten minutes the city's entire population had offered its assistance. Ford himself, however, took off the fan iron, went into the garage, repaired the fan iron and replaced the broken parts. This problem, coupled with a broken drive shaft on truck No. 1, being driven by Harry Linden with Kline aboard, set the schedule back three hours.

The temporarily disabled truck No. 1 was the commissary, which contained fried chicken and other goodies, so everyone had to forgo the noonday lunch. As afternoon wore on, a stop was made to telephone the Summit Hotel in Uniontown, Pennsylvania, for dinner reservations. Upon their arrival at the Summit Hotel it was announced that dinner would be served at once. Good food and rooms were provided, and while the campers were very much opposed to taking refuge in a hotel, it offered the welcome opportunity to get a bath and a shave.

In the evening Henry Ford insisted on climbing the mountain to get a view of Uniontown from its top, so, reluctantly but congenially, Harvey Firestone accompanied him on the hike. During the night truck No. 1 and the rest of the party arrived.

An early rise and an early breakfast made possible a prompt start August 20 toward the next objective, Keysers Ridge, Maryland, where DeLoach's mail awaited him. A mail stop there also gave Edison the opportunity to get a bottle of his favorite "pop," which

BELOW: *Firestone tries his hand at target shooting at Camp Hurley.*

was secured for him by Harvey junior. They pressed on to Oakland, making a stop on the way for lunch beside a beautiful stream and stand of large shade trees. Ford gave a little girl a dollar for a pail of apples, and after she joyfully skipped home, her father returned with a pail of cider which topped off the repast. Upon entering Oakland the vehicles were filled with gas and oil as Harvey junior proceeded to do Burroughs a favor by purchasing a box of caramels for him from the local candy shop. This so displeased Ford that he snatched up the box of candy and threw it up the street, much to the astonishment of the large group of locals who, as usual, had congregated around the cars.

Ford's knee-jerk reaction apparently stemmed from his protective stance toward the aged Burroughs, and his concern that Burroughs's health should not be adversely affected by such an indulgence. To the rest of the party, Burroughs was like a fragile and precious belonging, to be guarded with the utmost care. The trip was an extraordinary test of the endurance of a man of eighty, but he came through it in fine shape.

ABOVE: *Burroughs hits the bull's-eye at Camp Hurley near Greensburg.*

Driving was a pleasure on the seven miles of concrete highway on the way to Parsons, West Virginia, until a turnoff into some very rough and wild country brought back the familiar shaking and rattling. It was about 5 p.m. when Firestone and Edison drove along a small river, called Horse Shoe Run. About a half-mile from Leadmine, West Virginia, a picturesque camping site, with the mountains, a logging railroad and the river in the background, provided the perfect resting spot.

Camp was made on the banks of Horse Shoe Run. A smooth field across the road from the creek seemed attractive and Burroughs got the reluctant consent of the widow who owned it to pitch a camp there. Her patch of roasting ears of corn nearby made her hesitate; she had probably had experience with gypsy parties, and the magic names of Ford and Edison did not seem to impress her. But Edison was not attracted to the open field; the rough, grassy margin along the creek suited him better. And its proximity to the murmuring, eddying, rocky current appealed to the other campers, even though the mess tent had to be pitched astride a shallow gully and their individual tents elbowed each other in narrow spaces between the boulders.

Sighting of the nonpareil, a bird rarely seen north of the Potomac, gave Ford and Burroughs much pleasure as it was their first spotting of the species.

Dinner was prepared, and while they were eating in the gathering dusk, the residents of the lumbering camps and the mountaineers began to gather, forming an unusually rough-looking crowd. The crew and official photographer were somewhat alarmed and offered to remain up and guard the camp that night, Kline even showing his Smith and Wesson in his holster! But Ford convinced everyone that

BELOW: *Edison takes the wheel of the commissary truck at Greensburg, Pennsylvania, August 20.*

kind treatment would ensure perfect safety. "Peace" was made with the "enemy" by offering them cigars and handshakes. The result was a most congenial and hospitable group who offered to bring the logging engine down from their camp in the morning of August 21 for Edison. Edison hugely enjoyed being the engineer of the locomotive, to the delight of the motion picture photographer who filmed the event.

All the equipment was taken down and packed away for the start for Parsons. There being no road signs—and the farmlands and roadways looking very much alike—it was quite natural to get off the proper route. After driving down a mountain road, they found it necessary to drive back up the mountain before finally reaching Parsons, where gasoline and supplies were purchased. All the townspeople came into the drugstore to shake hands with the celebrities while Edison laid in a supply of chocolate. Ford gave advice and fixed a leaky waterjacket on the White truck.

After lunch it was on to Elkins, West Virginia, where the customary local group of Kodak people and autograph seekers welcomed everyone, while the mayor and some businessmen offered the hospitality of the Cheat Mountain Country Club, some twenty-five miles out, but still on the route. Almost immediately after starting out and just after passing through Beverly, the Simplex touring car sheared off a spring shackle bolt. After some persuasion Edison, Harvey Firestone, Jr., Burroughs and Professor DeLoach were dispatched to look for a camping place while Ford and Harvey Firestone, Sr., remained with the Simplex and one Ford auto. They spotted some farmers operating a threshing machine about three-quarters of a mile across a field. As luck would have it, Ford was able to find just the right bolt from the machine's toolbox. He thanked the farmers heartily, went back and fitted up the spring, with the entire repair

ABOVE: *Edison and Firestone take a break along the Lincoln Highway in Pennsylvania outside of Uniontown.*

LEFT: *The register of the Summit Hotel, Uniontown, Pennsylvania, with the signatures of the famous campers who stayed there on August 19, 1918.*

RIGHT: Noonday rest by the roadside, near Oakland, Maryland, August 20.

RIGHT: The overshot waterwheel of Evans's mill near Leadmine, West Virginia, provides a perfect prop for Edison, Harvey Firestone, Jr., Burroughs, Ford and Harvey Firestone, Sr. DeLoach is seated below.

RIGHT: The caravan stops for a noonday meal, August 20, on the way to set up camp at Horse Shoe Run, near Leadmine, West Virginia. Here campers and crew strike a rather formal pose.

delay amounting to about two hours. Then Ford and Harvey senior hurriedly drove over the mountains seeking their fellow campers. Dusk settled in. Finally, coming to a bridge, they spotted Harvey junior in the Packard, who guided them about one mile down the road to the campsite and on to the Cheat Mountain Country Club.

This was a surprise as Edison had absolutely refused to go to

LEFT: *The mess tent and commissary truck at the beautiful setting for the Horse Shoe Run camp, near Leadmine, West Virginia.*

LEFT: *The camping party in a relaxed mood. Edison and Burroughs are seated as the crew stands ready to serve.*

any club. A still greater surprise was the announcement that dinner would be served promptly within the hour, at 9:30 p.m. The night was cold and damp, so a fine, warm clubhouse with a big open fireplace was much more attractive than the camp along the river. The tenderfeet, who included Harvey junior and the crew, could not resist a hot bath and a comfortable bedroom that night, while the old-timers stuck to the camp.

The camp was on the banks of the Cheat River, a large, clear mountain trout brook on the grounds of the Cheat Mountain Country Club—an ideal spot. The walls of the main clubhouse were covered with paper outlines of big brook trout, telling a story of the rare sport the club members enjoyed, and apparently contradicting the river's name, "Cheat".

The mountains and valleys of the Virginias presented a marked contrast to those of Pennsylvania and New York. They had not been rubbed down and scooped out by the great glaciers; the valleys were markedly V-shaped rather than U-shaped. The valley sides were so steep that they were rarely cultivated; the farmland, for the most part, lay on the top of the broad, open river valley that held mile

BELOW: *Firestone and Edison in deep discussion in the dining tent at the Horse Shoe Run camp.*

ABOVE: *Harvey Firestone, Jr., Burroughs, a local logger, Ford, Edison and Harvey Firestone, Sr., pose before a steam-operated logging engine with its engineer in the cab near the Horse Shoe Run camp.*

after mile of beautiful farms producing hay, oats and buckwheat. We should also note here, to avoid confusion for those tracking on a map, that the trip through this part of the country, rich with spas and mineral waters, not only took the travelers through many towns with similar names–Warm Springs, Hot Springs, Sweet Springs, White Sulphur Springs–but also had them crossing and recrossing the state lines of Virginia, West Virginia, and Tennessee as they visited mountain villages situated right at the various borders.

After leaving Camp Cheat about 10 a.m. on August 22, Ford and Firestone, who as boys knew something about farmwork, stopped on Allegheny Mountain, near Bartow, West Virginia, where a farmer was cradling (cutting grain with a cradle scythe) on a hillside below the road. Ford and the farmer stood, with broad smiles on their faces, watching Firestone with his fingers on the cradle entangled in the oats and weeds. He, too, had a smile on his face. But cradling was not as easy as it looked. Ford had not forgotten his own cradling days on the farm in Michigan and proved to be quite proficient at it. Burroughs found himself at home when it came to raking and bundling the oats as he had done in Roxbury, New York.

The group enjoyed watching the friendly fun being scored by Edison, then had a tasty lunch laid out and ventured on in the direction of Warm Springs, Virginia. But they crossed the wrong bridge and journeyed up the mountain, landing in a small town called Bolar Springs. Upon inquiry, they found a place for their camp in a fine grove with warm springs and a bathing pool. The charge for a bath was fifteen cents.

At breakfast someone asked Edison if he would have prunes. "No," he replied, "I was once a telegraph operator and lived in a boardinghouse!" It was here that he gave several children who were

ABOVE: *Ford is the engineer for the logging engine at Horse Shoe Run camp, while Firestone serves as fireman and Edison fearlessly rides the cowcatcher.*

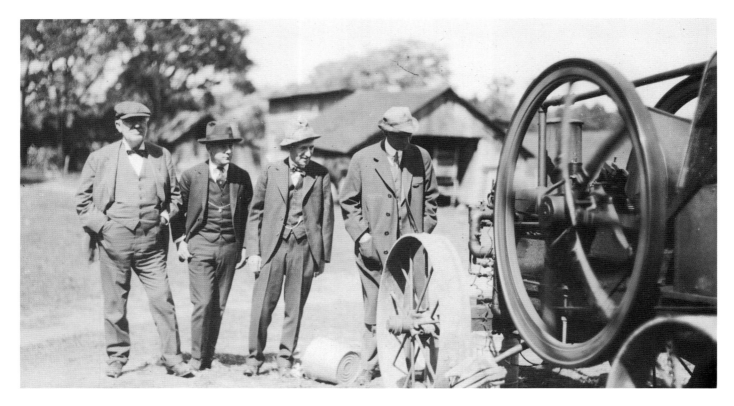

ABOVE: *Inspecting a threshing machine near Beverly, West Virginia, are Edison, DeLoach, Firestone and Ford.*

RIGHT: *Burroughs conducts a class in botany while awaiting minor repairs to the Simplex auto.*

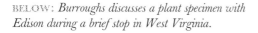

BELOW: *Burroughs discusses a plant specimen with Edison during a brief stop in West Virginia.*

standing about a nickel each. When asked if they knew his name, a little girl answered, "Yes, Mr. Gramophone."

The commissary was found to be short of bread since they had not yet reached Hot Springs, where restocking of supplies was assured. A call was made to the local general store, but no luck there. Up the hill was a hotel where the woman who came to the door said there was "none to spare." "Could you bake bread for us to have in the morning?" "Have no flour." "Will you consent to bake some if we furnish the flour?" "Yes," she responded to Harvey Firestone, who also mentioned how much Edison liked apple pie. Harvey junior and Kline placed a sack of flour on the commissary truck and delivered it to the hotel; that night the woman baked a few loaves of bread that were picked up by the hungry campers in the morning. She also baked a couple of apple pies and brought them to the camp just as they were finishing dinner. Edison insisted that some apple pie be saved for his breakfast. Great care was taken to secure it, but during the night the dogs got into the commissary truck and ate Edison's pie.

An incident occurred which lent itself to some friendly ribbing of Henry Ford. A salesman, presumably on his way to make a call in the next town, experienced an auto breakdown that drew Ford's attention. With screwdriver and pliers, he fixed the problem and soon had the anxious man ready to move on again. The man insisted on paying for the service, unaware of the identity of his famous repairman. Ford declined, saying something to the effect that he had enough money to last him many lifetimes. Skeptically, the man replied that Ford could not be very rich or he would not be riding in a Ford car! Of course, Edison did not let that slip by without comment.

The entire crew participated in an enjoyable afternoon, including a fifteen-cent bath that felt like a million dollars.

The next morning, August 23, they got off to a 9 a.m. start that resulted in their reaching Hot Springs by 11:15 a.m. and making an hour stopover at the homestead there. About seventeen miles out of Hot Springs they took a lunch break near a nice stream along the roadside. Here one of the crew shut off a watergate at a large concrete pool, which apparently was part of a waterpower system for a plant two miles distant. While lunch was being served, a man came up in a very bad frame of mind, complaining that his power had been shut off. After apologies were given and accepted, he advised them that the plant affected was the O. C. Barber phosphate plant,

ABOVE: *Ford, always on the alert for anything mechanical, and Firestone inspect the operation of a coal mine ventilator near their Camp Cheat in West Virginia.*

BELOW: *The Cheat Mountain, West Virginia, clubhouse where the campers found shelter and refreshment on a wet night, August 21.*

ABOVE: *Ford shows his skill in the cradling contest conducted in a local farmer's wheat field near Camp Cheat on Cheat Mountain, near Bartow, West Virginia.*

the most modern plant in the south. Firestone was drawn to inspect the plant and Ford to examine the waterpower. Following the inspections, they motored on to White Sulphur Springs, West Virginia. It was here that Harvey Firestone, attempting to secure a room at a hotel, went from one turndown to another before resigning himself to the fact that his appearance warranted a bath and a shave at the convenient bathhouse. While Ford and Professor DeLoach waited patiently, Edison and the crew went on to set up a very comfortable camp on the Tuckahoe River, a location which made it very easy to wash up in the morning.

After a good night's sleep the group moved out August 24 to the next objective, which was Narrows, Virginia. At Sweet Springs along the way there appeared to be many abandoned buildings, including summer hotels. Occupancy was said to be less than twenty-five percent. Apparently, the spring water was not very tasty. They stopped for lunch at Gap Mills, beside a small stream, where all the residents gathered to pay homage to them. Ford went to look at a mill, while one of the local citizens went to his home and returned with a can of maple syrup for Edison.

The countryside now became very rough and wild on the way to Narrows, Virginia, right on the border, which was a railroad center; the population, too, was rough and uncivilized, according to Firestone. A person who knew the countryside accompanied the crew out of town and helped locate a camping place at Wolf Creek near the narrows. This site proved to be one of the trip's best. A plus was the fact that no one knew who the campers were, nor did anyone inquire.

Firestone remarked to Edison, "This is the first place we have struck where they don't know any of us."

BELOW: *An amused farmer and Ford watch Firestone compete in the cradling contest.*

"Good," said Edison, "we shall have a good time here."

Camp was set up on a narrow, grassy margin of a broad, limpid creek in which the fish were jumping—a beautiful spot marred only by the proximity of the dusty public roadway. As an auto went by, a woman's voice was heard to exclaim, "What in hell is that?"

Provisions were in short supply and none were available in town, so Harvey junior and Kline drove through the countryside until they found chickens, fresh milk and eggs. Edison remarked that West Virginia had always been a rather hazy proposition to him and he was glad to get a clear impression of it; such was the case with all the travelers. They became quite familiar with this backbone of the Allegheny Mountains, which got folded and ruptured and mixed up in the building, with its elements unevenly distributed.

The next morning, August 25, Ford took his soap and towel to the creek and splashed around while washing up. The other three washed in cold water at a folding camp table. Then, while waiting for breakfast, they practiced target shooting—all except Edison. Burroughs, in spite of his more than four-score years, proved himself quite as good as the rest at this diversion. Breakfast consisted of oranges or bananas, cereal, eggs, toast, coffee and Burroughs's hot water. While they were eating in an open-ended dining tent, the cooks prepared sandwiches, fried chicken and other luncheon items. Loaded with these provisions against hunger, the passenger cars started on ahead, leaving the trucks to follow.

After a late start they encountered very bad roads, the heading being toward Bluefield, West Virginia, from Wolf Creek camp. Burroughs grew very tired, and with Professor DeLoach, boarded a train at Oakvale heading for Bluefield. Edison was persuaded by 1 p.m. to stop for lunch a short distance from Princeton. Ford took advan-

ABOVE: *The camping vehicles and their occupants ferry the Jackson River in Virginia on August 23.*

BELOW: *Edison enjoys a good story in the quiet solitude of the camp at Bolar Springs, Virginia, August 22.*

tage of the break to chat with a farmer there, picking up information about the surrounding farm country. The absence of bridges over the small streams was a novel southern feature. Edison called these fording places "Irish bridges."

At last there appeared the first macadam road they had encountered in many days as the procession advanced to Princeton, where they stopped for gasoline. From there it was on to Bluefield. The macadam was a blessing in more than one way as they had run out of tubes for the 38+7 pneumatic tires on the White truck.

John Burroughs and Professor DeLoach, who had gone ahead on the train and had already had dinner, met them at Bluefield. Harvey Firestone had ordered a tube to be shipped by parcel post, but the day being Sunday, the post office was closed. An appeal to the hotel proprietor prompted him to telephone a friend, who accommodated Firestone by answering his rap on the post office side door and handing over the emergency package.

They drove rather fast toward Tazewell, Virginia, as delays had made them anxious. They had become so used to the mountains where there were scarcely any roads at all that when they came to two roads they got lost. When they finally reached Tazewell the hour was late and Edison was nervous, so he drove on to find a camping site while Firestone remained behind to direct each vehicle as it came along. Since this took most of two hours, Firestone talked with the local citizens, including a circuit judge of West Virginia, as he waited. Finally, Sato, the cook, and Willmott arrived in a Ford car to pick him up. Along the way they encountered a party of young people from Bluefield who invited them to have lunch—not particularly for Firestone or Willmott, but for Sato, whose Japanese ancestry proved to be a novelty to the youths. Harvey junior and Ford

came by later and directed the three to their camp where dinner, somewhat later than usual, was prepared for them. Afterward, the Firestones took a walk and encountered some people singing and playing accordions. The father gave the son some music lessons on the accordion and pointed out what great pleasure and satisfaction there was to be had in living the simple country life.

By 10 a.m. the next day, August 26, the camp equipment was packed and a short run through Lebanon brought the caravan to its immediate objective of Hansonville, Virginia. The next six miles from there to Abingdon were so rough that Burroughs was forced to remark, rather emphatically, "These roads are the most damnable and despicable in the United States, probably built by the Germans as being one of their most cruel acts." However, after reaching Abingdon they struck paved roads again for their run into Bristol, Virginia-Tennessee, and found the contrast delightful.

The Hotel Bristol was the setting for a rather active lunchtime which began with a request for a table arrangement that would accommodate the full camping party. Not one of the hotel personnel immediately recognized these famous persons, so the request was dismissed out of hand by the head waiter, who said, "The tables are not large enough for such an arrangement. Take what is here or find lunch someplace else." But after they were seated and before they had ordered, word spread that it was Thomas Edison and other celebrities, and very quickly the tables were rearranged to their satisfaction. The head waiter even went to the kitchen to supervise the food preparation. When the meal was finished, the usual people gathered around, including the mayor of Bristol, local newspapermen, the Edison phonograph agent, the Ford agent and the Firestone agent, Charles J. Harkrader.

ABOVE: *Breakfast is served at the Bolar Springs camp, featuring everything from orange juice and milk to ham and eggs and toast and coffee. Hearty appetites are displayed by Edison, Firestone, Ford and Burroughs. The coats and ties add a formal touch.*

BELOW: *This plant supplied power to O. C. Barber's phosphate plant at a site seventeen miles from Hot Springs, Virginia. Here Barber is flanked by the Firestones and Ford.*

ABOVE: Firestone and Ford wade in a pool of the O. C. Barber phosphate plant in the mountains near Hot Springs, Virginia.

RIGHT: Campers and crew lunch on a gentle hillside beside a stream near Gap Mills, West Virginia, August 24.

Firestone and Ford went to the Firestone branch store, where pictures were taken and a 38+7 truck tire picked up, its having just arrived by express. It was on to the telegraph office to send a message to F. L. Seely at the Grove Park Inn, Asheville, North Carolina, notifying him that the travelers would arrive there Tuesday evening or Wednesday morning, and asking him to arrange for a camp on Sunset Mountain.

Back at the Hotel Bristol, W. H. Cox, a leading merchant, invited the party to stop at his farm, which was on their way, about ten miles out of the city. Upon their arrival, Cox introduced his wife and daughters to the visitors, pictures were taken and the trip was resumed to Elizabethton, Tennessee, where it started to rain quite heavily. They took refuge in a garage in town until the rain stopped, then moved on to Johnson City, where again a large crowd of people

ABOVE: *Wolf Creek, situated in the remote back country of Virginia near Narrows.*

ABOVE: *The camping party and crew having lunch at the J. W. Stinson farm near Princeton, West Virginia. Left to right: George Burns, a local farmer, Mr. Willmott, Frederick Ott, Ford, Firestone, Edison, Harvey Firestone, Jr., Mr. McNamara and Harry Linden.*

RIGHT: *Routine activity around camp in the farm fields at Tazewell, Virginia, August 25.*

BELOW: *An early morning washup at Camp Tazewell, near Witt, West Virginia, prepares Edison and Firestone for breakfast and another busy day.*

gathered. Not wanting to sit in their autos waiting for the rest of the caravan to arrive, they moved on toward Jonesborough, while Kline stayed behind to direct the stragglers.

Camp Robert E. Lee (named in honor of the Confederate general) was set up just two miles past Jonesborough, where a spring was found at the back of the home of a Mr. Lee (no relation to the general) in a field that was very difficult to enter. Access was through a barn, where Harry Linden tore off the top of his truck because the barn opening was not high enough to accommodate the vehicle. A pick and shovel had to be used to lower the truck enough to get it through the barn. The many cows and hogs in the barnyard presented an obvious obstacle to selecting a good site for the tents. Finally, a satisfactory site was chosen and Edison hired some boys, one of whom was the owner's son, Robert E. Lee, to gather firewood and run errands as

dusk started to fall and before the trucks began to arrive.

John Burroughs was somewhat tired, as the trip was beginning to wear on him, and he insisted on having his tent placed back in the field next to the woods and about a half mile away. He claimed the crew and the boys made too much noise, that they never went to bed and always woke him in the morning. He was anxious to pitch his tent before dusk and before the dew fell.

Dinner was served to hearty appetites, followed by the usual happy fellowship around a large and friendly campfire. Before long, searchlights began to shine over the hill, signaling the arrival of autos from Jonesborough, coming for the usual evening reception. The locals tried to impress the campers with stories about Jonesborough's being the oldest town in the state of Tennessee, and about their having Andrew Jackson's records and other Civil War era tales. This

ABOVE: *Watermelons were provided by visitors to Camp Robert E. Lee and the crew readily enjoyed them while changing a tire. Left to right: Harry Linden, R. V. Kline and Harold Sato.*

BELOW: *Sato, seated, and his crew during morning mess cleanup at Camp Robert E. Lee near Jonesborough, Tennessee, August 26.*

proved to be the happiest and most interesting evening of story telling and good cheer on the entire journey. Especially noteworthy was Thomas Edison's showing the women how the lights were installed in the tents and operated by batteries brought with him from Orange, New Jersey. The campers turned in about midnight.

During the evening John Burroughs had lamented that the camp was set up where the cattle could come up into his woods and bother him. They did indeed put in an appearance around camp—not only the cattle, but the hogs—and upset all the kitchen utensils and paraphernalia, which had to be speedily washed up for breakfast in the morning. Just as they finished breakfast, six or eight men from Jonesborough came up the field, each carrying a large watermelon for the campers.

Edison and Burroughs suffered the privation of scanty or delayed war news. Local papers, picked up here and there, gave brief summaries, while at the larger railroad towns they were able to get Cincinnati, Philadelphia or New York dailies, a day or two old.

Burroughs held informal botany classes for the campers along the way, pointing out the conspicuous roadside flowers, for hundreds of miles from Pennsylvania to North Carolina, eupatorium, or joe-pye weed, with its massive head of soft pinkish-purple, and the vivid purple ironweed—tall, stately, hardy flowers.

Camp was broken early on August 27 and the Jonesborough delegation informed the travelers that Asheville, North Carolina was

LEFT: *A partial view of Camp Robert E. Lee showing a lineup of caravan vehicles, the dining area and some of the tenting arrangement.*

eighty miles away. A route was made up for each car with instructions to meet at the Grove Park Inn in Asheville, where they would decide whether time would permit their setting up camp or whether they should stay at the inn. A stay at the inn was anathema to Edison, who said he had had reservations there for three weeks some time before, but stayed only two weeks because he got tired of changing his clothes for the dining room.

Harvey junior's car contained Ford, Burroughs and Professor DeLoach. Edison had Kline and Firestone for riding companions as the caravan headed out for Asheville. The autos were nearly out of

ABOVE: *Ford visits with Sam Kirkpatrick, W. P. Shipley and friends at Camp Robert E. Lee near Jonesborough, Tennessee.*

ABOVE: *Ford and Edison never failed to inspect anything related to waterpower. Here they stand to the left of the overshot waterwheel of an abandoned mill near Weaverville, Tennessee, as Burroughs and Firestone stand to the right.*

gasoline when they pulled up to a store pump in a remote village about ten miles from Greeneville, but the storekeeper, too, was almost out of gasoline. Urgent solicitation was required to entice him to part with three gallons, just enough for their run into Greeneville.

Word had been telephoned ahead that some important people would be arriving there soon, so immediately after they arrived at the first garage for fuel, a very large crowd gathered. The usual invitations were issued to see the important town sites, but Firestone, with tact and diplomacy, convinced the townspeople of their urgent need to leave, as time was short and Edison impatient. The mayor and chief of police escorted them out of town—this time it was an honor—although in the haste, Firestone became separated from the others.

The weather was exceedingly hot and humid in the small town of Newport when Firestone spotted the company's Packard car standing in front of a hotel where the rest of the party was already having lunch with some local threshers. The landlady persuaded the crowd in the dining room to move so that Firestone and Edison could be seated next to Ford and Burroughs. She was more interested in Burroughs than in the others, so Ford, also favorably impressed by her, promised to send a set of Burroughs's books as a present. After dinner Edison, as usual, went into a room, sat down and read his paper, as the citizens gathered around to look at him or get his autograph, while Ford, also as usual, mingled with the crowd.

After leaving Newport they experienced very rough roads and mountainous country before arriving at Hot Springs, North Carolina. Some persuasion was necessary for Firestone to get Edison to agree to visit a nearby German prisoner-of-war camp, where an army colonel guided them through. The camp housed approximately twenty-two hundred men, mostly sailors from interned German ships, who had been there since the outbreak of the war. Their trek continued to Mars Hill, with the road climbing and descending through towns along the way for a tortuous twenty-five miles more.

ABOVE: *The party is greeted by F. L. Seely at the Grove Park Inn, Asheville, North Carolina, August 27. Burroughs and DeLoach left the group at this point and returned home by train. Edison, Ford, and the Firestones returned by motor car.*

LEFT: *The lobby of the Grove Park Inn, Asheville, North Carolina, where the weary travelers were graciously hosted by F. L. Seely on August 27.*

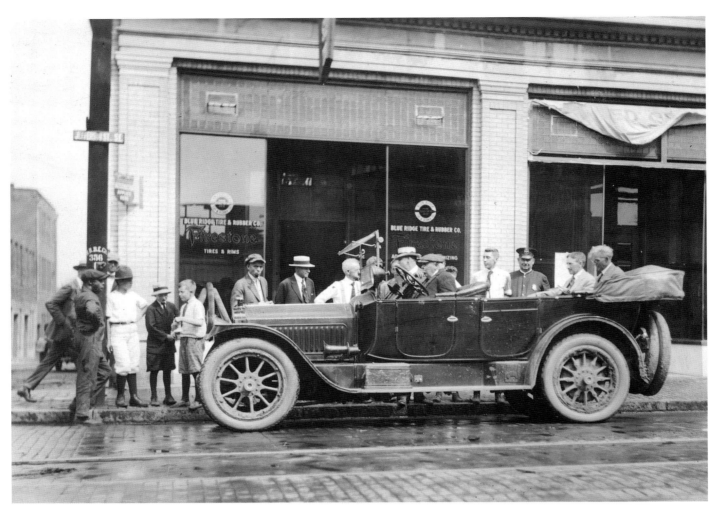

Firestone, taking no chances, changed seats with his companions every time the side of the mountain changed. In other words, as Edison said, "He always wanted an inside room when the drop was too far and the slope too steep." Or he just stood outside on the running board of the auto.

They finally reached Mars Hill, where there happened to be a small college with its service flag–containing 128 stars representing enlistments from the college–hanging in the street. Children and college girls presented flowers and fruit to their illustrious guests, who were asked to address the assemblage. Edison placated the crowd by rising up in his usual gallant way and bowing toward each side of the auto, after which the campers moved on toward Weaverville, North Carolina.

Before reaching their trip's next objective, Firestone finally had to tell Edison about the possibility of their having to stay at the Grove Park Inn in Asheville, North Carolina. If, however, Edison wanted to camp, they could stop and wait for the trucks. Edison consented to go on to Asheville.

In Weaverville the president of a local college came up, shook hands and introduced a number of local citizens to the campers. The women had a Red Cross booth set up across the street and urged the group to come in and have tea, but Edison graciously declined. He also passed on a request to speak, instead offering up Firestone.

LEFT: *The travelers arrive for an overnight stay at the Hotel Huffy in Hickory, North Carolina, while motoring back to Hagerstown, Maryland.*

Whereupon the college president jumped onto the auto and introduced Firestone, who promptly offered a few words to those assembled. Subsequently, the travelers had a comfortable and leisurely drive into Asheville, where at 8:30 p.m. they were greeted cordially by F. L. Seely, who had all their accommodations ready. Edison lamented that his grip and wardrobe had not arrived, so that he could not shave and put on a clean collar. But he was most congenial as a fine dinner was served in the dining room—a room he insisted was practically the same as the camp dining facilities. The party took motion pictures and later Edison read until midnight, keeping everyone in the hotel up until he finally decided to retire.

The next morning, August 28, after a 10 a.m. breakfast, Firestone and Ford took a long walk over the adjacent golf links and up Sunset Mountain. Upon returning they had a talk with Edison and it was decided that they would tour back home and leave the camping outfit to find its own way home. Burroughs, as the senior member of the party, had had his share of excitement, enjoyment and exposure at this juncture, so he bade farewell and bon voyage to the others as he boarded a passenger train, along with Professor DeLoach, for his beloved Catskill Mountain retreat. After lunch, Kodak and motion pictures were taken in front of the inn, and the travelers departed for Hickory, North Carolina, in Harvey junior's car—Edison in the front seat, Firestone and Ford in the rear seat.

It was 3 p.m., with rain pouring down, when they started out of Asheville for their destination ninety-six miles away. Along the route they stopped at a hotel for supper in the little town of Marion. Upon their departure from the town, and just as dusk was setting in, a spring broke on the auto. Ford again brought his mechanical genius into play with some cord, and who knows what else, to repair the damaged spring, thereby permitting the tour to resume. Before they reached Hickory, a piloting party came out to greet them. The trav-

ABOVE: *Dinner was served and a night's lodging secured for the threesome at the Broad Street Hotel in Martinsville, Virginia, August 29. This stopover created such excitement in the town that on returning from a stroll about the community they found reentry to the hotel almost impossible.*

Grove Park Inn, Asheville, N. C.

Absolutely Fireproof   Open all the Year

The Finest Resort Hotel in the World

August 28th 1918.

Biltmore Industries

Hand Weaving and Hand-Carved Woodwork

Biltmore Industries had its beginning in the year 1901, in an industrial school started in Biltmore Village under the patronage of Mrs. George W. Vanderbilt.

The enterprise so far outgrew its early surroundings that in 1917 Mrs. Vanderbilt sold it in its entirety to Mr. F. L. Seely, who built and operates Grove Park Inn.

Unique Old English shop buildings have been built on the grounds of the Inn, and the Industries, with all its workers, moved into its new home — some three miles from the place of its birth.

The same workers are employed, and the products are being made as they have been made from the beginning.

Every piece of Biltmore Homespun is guaranteed to contain absolutely nothing but new sheep's wool. The colors are guaranteed, and it is guaranteed not to shrink.

All hand-carved woodwork is guaranteed, and any pieces not perfect will be replaced or the money refunded.

Dear Mr. Seely—

After a ten days camping trip thro' the mountains of West Virginia and your own "Land of the Sky". We felt when we arrived at Grove Park Inn, the "Finest Resort Hotel in the world", that possibly we were not quite presentable enough to expect a welcome.

We not only received the welcome but the warmest hospitality we have ever had extended to us.

May you live long and be a blessing to many other travelers—!

John Burroughs   Thos A Edison

R J H   Harvey S. Firestone

Harvey S. Firestone, Jr.   Henry Ford

ABOVE: *Upon departing the Grove Park Inn the six party members addressed a note to Seeley: "When we arrived—possibly we were not quite presentable enough to expect a welcome. We not only received the welcome but the warmest hospitality we have ever had extended to us."*

LEFT: *The Forsythe Country Club in Winston-Salem, where the travelers were ceremoniously treated to a royal lunch by the Rotary Club.*

elers were grateful because, in the dark, and without guidance, they never would have found the hotel. Everyone registered at the Hotel Huffy: two rooms with a bath between for Ford and Edison and a room and bath downstairs for Firestone. This room had the kitchen on one side and the office on the other. At about 3 a.m. the cleaning crew began to sweep up in the office. The activity disturbed Firestone, and a half hour later he jumped out of bed, went into the office in his nightshirt and insisted that the janitor clean the room later in the morning. But when he returned to bed, in hopes of a nice, peaceful slumber until daybreak, the kitchen began to stir. So much for a restful night's sleep.

Upon arising, August 29, everyone had breakfast together, then went outside for the usual reception, which included a Mr. Bolick, who had been a Ford agent for the past fifteen years and hailed from Conover, about fifteen miles from Hickory.

The next stop was in Statesville, where Ford advised that he needed more material to properly repair the spring. This was obtained while Harvey junior telephoned ahead to the Winston-Salem Firestone branch, asking them to have a spring ready for him upon his arrival there. The locals had, by this time, gathered around, but the travelers accommodated them only briefly before moving on. Their luck did not hold out, and five miles from town the auto spring gave way again. The necessary readjustment took over an hour, which gave Firestone an opportunity to circulate among the local people, as was his custom, making inquiries and getting an idea of their lifestyles. He spoke with a "colored" family who owned forty acres of land, rented forty more, and had eleven children, two of them married. They had a fine cotton field, and their accomplishments and manners created a rather favorable impression on Firestone.

ABOVE: *Another overshot waterwheel of an abandoned gristmill is examined by Firestone and Ford, this time near Lexington, Virginia.*

With the spring repaired, it was now possible to move on to lunch in Mocksville, North Carolina. However, upon arriving there at noon, the touring group was met by the local citizens who, very

ABOVE: *A large crowd greeted the campers on their arrival at Winston-Salem, North Carolina. Ivar Simpson is at the wheel of the right-hand-drive Simplex auto, with Edison by his side. Firestone is seated behind them.*

politely, advised them that Winston-Salem, thirty miles farther on, had a luncheon almost ready. Back on the road again, they were met twenty miles from Winston-Salem by some six cars of leading citizens ready to show the way into the city. Out of consideration for his touring companions, Firestone got out of the auto in which he was riding and into a following car so that one of the greeting party could replace him and act as pilot. Harvey junior, being quite hungry, drove at a fast clip, leaving the others in the dust. Eventually everyone landed at the Forsythe Country Club, only to discover that the luncheon was just being prepared. An hour of visiting on the large club porch was followed by a rather formal "state" luncheon in the clubhouse.

Following this afternoon meal, the usual pictures were taken, then a drive into the city brought them to a large reception at the Ford Motor Company branch, after which the tour headed for Martinsville, Virginia. Along the way the road became quite muddy and the auto settled in. Ford and Edison insisted that the car be jacked up and extracted in that manner. But Firestone, who had more faith in a team of mules, went down the road to secure them from a farmer. They borrowed a chain from a woman, untying it from a tree where it tethered her cow, and hitched the team to the car. This did the trick, as the mules easily pulled the car out of its entrapment to land it on solid ground again.

Upon returning the cow chain, Ford noticed that the woman's teeth were missing and that one of her children was sickly and crippled. At this point a man, his wife and two children came along, having heard that Ford was in Winston-Salem. The man was a former Ford dealer who wanted to meet Henry Ford. This gave Ford an opportunity to provide for the welfare of the woman who had so graciously supplied the tow chain. Ford, who had already given her twenty-five dollars, made arrangements with the former Ford dealer to supervise the woman's dental work and her disabled child's hospitalization, with Ford paying the costs. A further request was made of the woman: it would be appreciated if she would remain there and guide the other vehicles around the quagmire as they approached.

Upon rolling into Martinsville, they found a large reception committee congregated at the Broad Street Hotel, many of the women dressed all in white. The main concern, however, was dinner, which, as it happened, was served immediately in the hotel dining room, with the doors closed to keep out the crowd. This proved to be the first place on the entire trip where contributions were solicited: two young women asked for and received a donation for the Red Cross. With the evening meal finished, the travelers wandered outside and were beseeched to join the group at the motion-picture show. This invitation was politely turned down. The crowd now was so large that it was almost impossible to reenter the hotel. The party retired quite early, only to find in the morning, August 30, another large

ABOVE: *Harvey Firestone, Jr., and Ford explore the stream at the base of the Natural Bridge in Virginia, August 29.*

reception prepared for them. It was here that Firestone became particularly interested in Marshall Field's fabric mill and establishment. He talked to the manager, who took the group out to inspect the operation and explain its functions and objectives. The company brought mountaineers in at a reasonable wage, furnished nice homes for rent at one dollar per month for each room and also provided schools, churches and amusements.

Firestone stopped at his branch store upon arriving in Roanoke, Virginia, inquiring of his agent where the best hotel accommodations could be found and requesting him to advise Kline, with the Simplex auto, and Sato and Willmott, with the Ford auto, to proceed to that hotel. A midday rest was in order, then lunch. Later, while on a search for a tube and gasoline, the auto ran out of fuel, whereupon Firestone commandeered a horse and wagon to bring enough gasoline to get the vehicle to a filling station. While leaving Roanoke, they encountered a car whose driver apparently wanted to pilot the tour out of the city. Not caring to have this occur, the travelers passed the newcomers' car, whereupon a race ensued for about five miles, with speeds reaching more than sixty miles per hour, as the would-be pilot tried to retake the lead. This was not pleasing to Ford or Edison, but Firestone had enough sporting blood to instruct Harvey junior to keep ahead of them.

Natural Bridge, Virginia, was reached as the afternoon wore on. Ford, Firestone and Harvey junior paid one dollar each, registered and

went down to look at the bridge while Edison remained in the auto. The hour was 5 p.m. when the three men followed the trail under Natural Bridge to a cave and lost river, along with some other points of interest. A delegation from the hotel met them as they returned, and escorted the threesome back to the auto. By now it was 7 p.m., and Ford and Edison were itchy to be on their way over the mountains to where dinner should be waiting for them, about fourteen miles away. Firestone, after some persuasion, got the others to agree to remain at Natural Bridge Hotel for dinner, which would then land the travelers in Lexington, Virginia, after people had retired, thus eliminating the annoyance of a welcoming crowd. The proprietor furnished front rooms where they could wash up, and a band to escort them to the dining room, where royal treatment and a later reception proved to be quite enjoyable before they departed for Lexington.

Rooms had been reserved at the Castle Inn in Lexington. The inn was in the mountains about a half mile from the city and was somewhat difficult to locate at night. They were escorted to their rooms, then joined a welcoming group congregated on the front porch. But here a rivalry developed between hostesses, each wanting the distinguished men as their guests of honor. One woman was giving a dancing party and invited Firestone because, she reasoned, quite rightly, that he would bring his son, Harvey junior, along. Ford and Edison attended the other women's Bevo (soft drink) and cheese party on the porch. A very enjoyable evening was experienced by all, after which they retired for the night.

Breakfast was ordered for 7 a.m., August 31, a special breakfast for these special travelers. However, the other guests of Castle Inn were in the lobby and reception room bright and early, ready to participate in a reception complete with picture-taking.

Edison's chauffeur and Willmott, who was riding with him, had been unable to locate the party in Lexington the night before and had driven on to Staunton, Virginia. They made contact by telephone and received instructions to wait there, and the rest of the party would meet them. On the way, the president of Washington and Lee University escorted the party through the university, including in the tour the tomb of Robert E. Lee and Lee's office, which was preserved just as he had left it.

At Staunton, the wayward auto with its occupants was located. After purchasing gasoline and a few items they took to the road again, with a stop along the way for lunch. The secretary of a local fair association came into the room to see whether anyone would come out to the fair and hear a senator speak, but Ford declined for the group.

After lunch, they walked down the street to the store of Edison's agent, where a large delegation had gathered to meet them. After twenty minutes or so, they drove on to Winchester, Virginia. It was

ABOVE: *To avoid the gathering hordes of admirers, driver Ivar Simpson takes the travelers, after lunch at the Hamilton Hotel, to a spot outside Hagerstown, Maryland, for their final good-byes.*

raining when Winchester came into view, so they stopped at a garage where they could more comfortably raise the top of the car. Firestone called on his agent at his branch store for a few minutes while Edison insisted on having an ice-cream soda in a nearby store. Their stay in Winchester was short, allowing for an early start toward Hagerstown, Maryland, their final destination. Between Staunton and Winchester they passed through nineteen tollgates. This just happened to be the last day the tollgates were in operation; they closed the following day.

This entire final stretch run from Roanoke to Hagerstown, took them parallel to the Appalachian trail and along the spine of the Blue Ridge Mountains—the route that today is Interstate 81.

They reached Hagerstown at 7 p.m., just in time to register at the Hamilton Hotel and have dinner. In the evening Ford and Firestone took a walk around town, with the latter commenting that the fifty-cent pair of wool socks he was wearing was the best he had ever purchased, their usual cost being two dollars. Following the walk the two went to Edison's room, where he had been asleep. They read as they sat there, then visited, talking about the magic moments of the trip, and had a happy and congenial last evening together. All regretted that in the morning each would be going his separate way.

The next morning, September 1, to avoid attracting the usual attention when saying good-bye, they drove several miles out of Hagerstown after breakfast, before taking Kodak and motion pictures of the touring party. At noon Edison started for Orange, New Jersey, and Ford and Firestone, with Harvey junior, made their way to Pittsburgh. Sato and Willmott followed in the Ford car as the 1918 camping trip came to a close.

THE OP

NO ROAD

1919

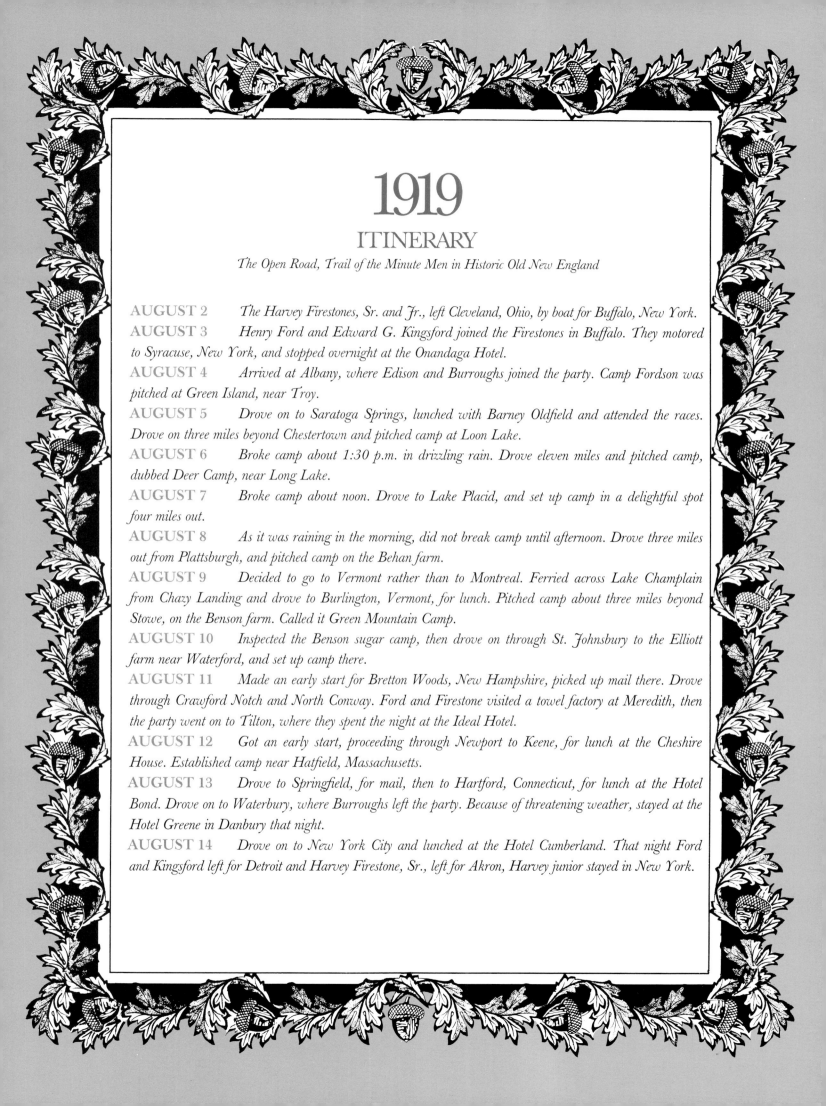

1919

ITINERARY

The Open Road, Trail of the Minute Men in Historic Old New England

AUGUST 2   *The Harvey Firestones, Sr. and Jr., left Cleveland, Ohio, by boat for Buffalo, New York.*

AUGUST 3   *Henry Ford and Edward G. Kingsford joined the Firestones in Buffalo. They motored to Syracuse, New York, and stopped overnight at the Onandaga Hotel.*

AUGUST 4   *Arrived at Albany, where Edison and Burroughs joined the party. Camp Fordson was pitched at Green Island, near Troy.*

AUGUST 5   *Drove on to Saratoga Springs, lunched with Barney Oldfield and attended the races. Drove on three miles beyond Chestertown and pitched camp at Loon Lake.*

AUGUST 6   *Broke camp about 1:30 p.m. in drizzling rain. Drove eleven miles and pitched camp, dubbed Deer Camp, near Long Lake.*

AUGUST 7   *Broke camp about noon. Drove to Lake Placid, and set up camp in a delightful spot four miles out.*

AUGUST 8   *As it was raining in the morning, did not break camp until afternoon. Drove three miles out from Plattsburgh, and pitched camp on the Behan farm.*

AUGUST 9   *Decided to go to Vermont rather than to Montreal. Ferried across Lake Champlain from Chazy Landing and drove to Burlington, Vermont, for lunch. Pitched camp about three miles beyond Stowe, on the Benson farm. Called it Green Mountain Camp.*

AUGUST 10   *Inspected the Benson sugar camp, then drove on through St. Johnsbury to the Elliott farm near Waterford, and set up camp there.*

AUGUST 11   *Made an early start for Bretton Woods, New Hampshire, picked up mail there. Drove through Crawford Notch and North Conway. Ford and Firestone visited a towel factory at Meredith, then the party went on to Tilton, where they spent the night at the Ideal Hotel.*

AUGUST 12   *Got an early start, proceeding through Newport to Keene, for lunch at the Cheshire House. Established camp near Hatfield, Massachusetts.*

AUGUST 13   *Drove to Springfield, for mail, then to Hartford, Connecticut, for lunch at the Hotel Bond. Drove on to Waterbury, where Burroughs left the party. Because of threatening weather, stayed at the Hotel Greene in Danbury that night.*

AUGUST 14   *Drove on to New York City and lunched at the Hotel Cumberland. That night Ford and Kingsford left for Detroit and Harvey Firestone, Sr., left for Akron, Harvey junior stayed in New York.*

ABOVE: *Burroughs is the center of attention as visitors from the neighborhood call on the campers in the evening at the Loon Lake camp, August 5.*

1919

THE OPEN ROAD

"Trail of the Minute Men in Historic Old New England"

Their 1919 venture on the open road took the campers through some of the most beautiful parts of New England, covering more than eleven hundred miles during their eleven-day outing. All the members of the 1918 expedition were along: Thomas Edison, Henry Ford, John Burroughs, Harvey Firestone and his son, Harvey junior.

Ford brought his camp equipment by night boat over Lake Erie from Detroit, Michigan, to Buffalo, New York, on Sunday, August 3. Edward G. Kingsford, manager of the Ford Motor Company's holdings on Michigan's Upper Peninsula, accompanied him. Everything was new for this trip. One of Ford's personal—as well as business—fundamentals was to have everything absolutely clean and in place. He had two cars fitted out, enamel and nickel shining, just the way he liked to have everything, including the machinery in his shop. Car A, or the "kitchen cabinet car," on a Ford chassis, was as fully furnished a kitchen and pantry, including a water tank below, as he could devise. Planning this equipment was a fun project and a nice diversion from his recent grinding war effort.

On the running board was a large gasoline stove fed from the motor tank, and inside the car was a built-in icebox and compartments for every kind of food needed for camping. It was so tightly fitted it could attain a speed of forty miles per hour without a rattle. Harold Sato, the chef, drove this vehicle.

Car B, a Cadillac, was outfitted with the camping gear and was driven by Fred W. Loskowski, a muscular army veteran of the recent war, who was charged by Mr. Dahlinger of the Ford Motor Company "to be sure everything was OK and nobody bothered the Boss, nor the rest of them." Most of the tents were eight by eight feet or ten by ten feet, with sides that rolled up, a floor and a mosquito netting flap in front. Loskowski would set these tents up along with a twenty by twenty foot dining tent, complete with a round dining table and Lazy Susan. When a camper wanted to pass something he just spun the Lazy Susan

ABOVE: *Ford chisels his initials into the future corner-stone for the Fordson tractor plant at the Green Island hydroelectric site on August 5. Edison is holding his cap; Firestone stands behind Ford; next on the right is Burroughs; on Burroughs' left is Cornelius Burns, mayor of Troy, New York; James R. Watt, mayor of Albany, New York, is standing between Edison and Ford. The other three principal campers followed suit by adding their initials to the cornerstone.*

BELOW: *At left, Mayor Burns of Troy, New York, next to Edison, center, and Mayor Watt of Albany, watch the cornerstone ceremonies of the proposed Fordson tractor plant at Green Island, New York, August 5.*

until the item reached its destination. Potatoes on the other side? Just turn the Lazy Susan to get them.

Car C, a Ford touring car, was driven by George Ebbing, who also doubled as the camp photographer. Jimmy Smith drove Ford's car.

The Firestones traveled from Akron, Ohio, to Cleveland, where they dined at the Hollenden Hotel before they boarded the ferry at 8 p.m., August 2, for the Lake Erie voyage to Buffalo, in quite favorable weather. By some good fortune they were able to secure the luxurious President's Stateroom, with its private deck which they enjoyed to the utmost. On disembarking, August 3, they proceeded directly to the Buffalo Club, where breakfast was served with a Mr. Rodgers and another prominent banker as guests. Immediately after eating, Harvey junior drove down to the Detroit and Buffalo docks to meet Ford and Kingsford as they arrived. Back at the Buffalo Club, where Ford and Kingsford breakfasted, the party assembled for an 11 a.m. start. They drove sixty-three miles to the Avon Inn for lunch. The six-car assembly continued east at a leisurely pace and arrived in Syracuse, at seven in the evening. The party stopped at the Onandaga Hotel for dinner on the Roof Garden, then spent the evening chatting and reading before retiring at 10:30 p.m.

Everyone was up for an 8:30 a.m. breakfast in the Grill Room on August 4. During the night the newspapers had gotten word of their arrival and several reporters were on hand for interviews. As Ford and Firestone started for the Firestone Company branch store, where the trucks and cars had been stored for the night, they were surrounded by a crowd, with newspaper photographers running after them, taking pictures at almost every step.

Finally the party was able to assemble at the branch store and set out for Albany, New York, 150 miles away. The drive was a pleasant one, without incident, the caravan arriving about five in the afternoon for their rendezvous with Edison and Burroughs. Edison, who was driving his car from Orange, New Jersey, had not arrived as yet, but Burroughs had, having taken the train from his home in the Catskills. After his experience in Syracuse, Ford did not care to wait around the hotel, so he and Burroughs, driven by Harvey junior, went out to Green Island, just outside of Troy, New York, where Ford had purchased a large tract of land to build a tractor plant. Firestone waited for Edison in Albany.

Upon arriving at Green Island, Ford and Burroughs found that the faithful crew had pitched the tents, installed the lights and had everything in first-class shape. Ford planned to build a hydroelectric plant here, where the government had built a dam across the Hudson River for some war purpose; rather than see this power go to waste, he had leased the rights for his proposed Fordson tractor plant. Edison and Ford, if it were possible, would have dammed every suitable stream in the country just to get the power. It is doubtful that, when passing an old abandoned mill, they ever failed to measure the force of the stream or talk about putting the wasted power to work. Ford had purchased seven abandoned mill sites on the River Rouge near his Detroit factory and fitted them with water turbines to furnish power to various factory units. Plans had not been formulated for a factory at Green Island, but nevertheless he picked out a future cornerstone and had each party member chisel his initials on it the next day.

Edison finally arrived in Albany in time to have dinner with Firestone at the Ten Eyck Hotel, after which they journeyed out to Green Island to join their other two campmates. A hearty welcome greeted Edison upon his arrival in camp, then the evening was spent around the campfire chatting and telling stories.

The next morning, August 5, the campers rose bright and early and did justice to a fine breakfast. The morning hours were spent in more or less formal ceremonies preparing the cornerstone for the proposed Fordson tractor plant. Mayor Watt of Albany and a party of prominent men journeyed out to meet the campers and welcome them to that part of New York State. As each of the four campers chiseled his initials in the cornerstone, pictures were taken; then the waterpower site was inspected. The tires on the Ford cars were exchanged for oversize tires to ensure easier riding for the culinary outfit, and at 11:30 a.m. the camp paraphernalia was finally loaded in its van and the whole party was ready for the open road.

ABOVE: *Driver George Ebbing surveys the early morning breakfast activity at the Loon Lake camp.*

Saratoga Springs, New York, where the summer race meeting was in full swing, attended by thousands of visitors, was the setting for the midday meal with Barney Oldfield, the famous auto racer. He was a personal friend of Ford's, who invited him to be their luncheon guest. After dining at the Grand Union Hotel the campers went to the race-track, viewed the horseraces from over the fence and stayed just a short while before heading to Loon Lake, about three miles beyond Chestertown, New York, where they pitched camp at lakeside.

Loskowski, with the help of Edison's and Firestone's chauffeurs, staked out the tents, each with a camper's nametag attached, put lights in and equipped each with a folding cot, mattress, blankets, pillows, sheets, everything for the campers' comfort. Meanwhile, Sato had set up the commissary and had started dinner with the help of Jimmy Smith. Later Loskowski also pitched in to help. Ford was busy chopping wood and starting a campfire. This included setting up two iron bars which extended over the fire and to which hooks were attached to support the cooking pots. Loskowski would recall later:

"Mr. Ford, he would always have an axe and would go and get some kindling wood. He wanted a fire, regardless of how hot it was—he wanted a campfire. Mr. Ford was more active than the others. He was almost like one of us guys, if you could have seen him around there! You would never [have] thought of him as Mr. Ford if you could have seen him, I'll tell you the truth about that. He used to get a kick out of Firestone. He used to kid the hell out of Firestone for taking a bath, having to stop at a hotel to take a bath! I woke up one morning and got up, thinking to straighten things up around there. We were staying at some falls up in there. I looked down the hill, and there was the Boss. He was washing in his undershirt. He had some soap and was washing himself all over. Cold? The water was cold, but it didn't make any difference to him. He came up and I was

LEFT: *Morning dawns on a neat row of the campers' tents at Deer camp, near Long Lake, New York, August 6.*

standing there. He said, 'Boy, that feels good! Why don't you go down and get one?' So I took one. Yep, great old fellow!"

The Loon Lake camp gave the party its first real taste of camp-life. Burroughs selected a special site for his tent, pitching it close to a small waterfall, claiming the sound of falling water was a great aid to his sleep. However, a damp chill at night usually accompanied this type of camp location. Burroughs's tent was set up first, as he was usually tired after the day's ride. His evening meal, too, had to be an early and plain one, that being his habit. So, after a simple repast of toast and hot water he would turn in, and by the time the rest were sitting down to a hearty supper he would usually be sound asleep. In the evening the party gathered around the campfire, where Edison entertained with his vast storehouse of information on various topics. He always carried a good supply of books and reading material wherever he went. Loskowski remembered these campfires:

"They were just like a bunch of kids when they were together, more and more like kids. I used to get a kick out of them! The old man [Ford] would talk pretty loud to Mr. Edison. Of course, Firestone—they used to kid him about his tires. In their conversations they used to kid one another quite a bit. We could hear their conversations, but if they were around a fire, we used to keep far enough away; we didn't want to butt into their business. No one person would do the most talking. There was quite a bit of talking amongst the three of them—Ford, Firestone and Edison. Mr. Kingsford, he seldom said much. Mr. Burroughs, he was kind of quiet. Old Edison and Mr. Ford, they'd really talk. Of course, Mr. Firestone would have to butt in once in a while and tell them how rotten the Ford was! They'd kid him about his tires. I've never seen a bunch of fellows—you know, big guys with money—have more fun than they did. They were just like a bunch of kids when they went on those trips. Yes sir, those were really times. If those times were back now, I'd go, as crippled as I am. Wonderful times—nobody in the world could have better trips than those trips."

Occasionally around the campfire they were able to draw Edison

BELOW: *The beauty of the creek and hardwood trees appealed to the campers at the Loon Lake camp.*

ABOVE: *Firestone, Burroughs, Ford and Edward G. Kingsford find the raspberries quite plentiful enough for a delicious shortcake at Deer camp.*

ABOVE: *A Ford car outfitted with kitchen utensils comes in handy as breakfast is prepared on the Elliott farm, near Waterford, Connecticut, August 10.*

out on chemical problems, and he would reel off formula after formula as though he were reading from a book. As a practical chemist he perhaps had few equals in the country.

They carried no cards or any other games, nor did the occasion arise for their use. Neither Ford nor Burroughs smoked. Edison and Firestone did, but they did not produce their cigars until evening.

During the night it rained, and when the morning of August 6 dawned it was still drizzling. This made it impractical to break camp because the crew did not want to pack the tents while they were wet. Clearing weather in the midmorning allowed the gear to be packed, and by 1:30 p.m. the party was on the way again, headed north. Two hours later a roadside stop was made for lunch from a basket of sandwiches prepared earlier by Sato. Loskowski's words describe an interesting point about the informality that prevailed on these excursions:

"When we drove along, Mr. Ford was in the lead. I was the last man, always behind. I remember one day on that trip when I got a flat tire. They left me. God knows what road he was going to take! Nobody knows, only Mr. Ford himself [and Edison]. They had gone, and I changed tires and got it going. I was driving the Cadillac on that trip. I was coming down this main pike just balling her, trying to catch up. I didn't know which way they was going. There might be a fork in the road, and they might take the right fork or the left fork. It was near lunchtime. They had pulled alongside of the road. They had come down a hill and gone up a hill, quite a steep hill. They stopped there to eat lunch. Mr. Edison used to call me 'the Swede.' He said, 'I wonder where the Swede is?' He always talked pretty loud. Mr. Ford says, 'Don't worry about that Swede, he'll find us—here he comes!' They could hear that old motor, just a-roaring. Boy, I got to that hill and I could see them stopped. Boy, I had an

ABOVE: *A restful noontide was enjoyed by the campers after a hearty lunch on the way to Lake Placid, New York. Crew members wait patiently at left, August 7.*

awful time stopping, I'm going to tell you, 'cause I had quite a load on! Mr. Ford says, 'I told you he would be here!' The Boss came over and wanted to know what was the matter. I told him I had a flat tire and had to change it."

After passing through Long Lake, New York, they encountered some very bad roads, and as darkness approached they pitched camp in the wilderness about eleven miles farther on. Two things made this camp very favorable: one was the sparkling beauty, the other was the absence of visitors. Red raspberries were abundant at this time of year, so the crew gathered enough for Sato to make raspberry shortcake for the dinner. A number of deer were spotted, a marvel for these city-dwellers, which prompted them to christen the camp Deer camp. The sleeping tents were back in the woods, the mess tent close to the roadside, and the bonfire just across the road. Camaraderie around a roaring fire topped off a pleasant evening. The pine-scented air combined with the solitude of the forest induced a sound and restful sleep.

Loskowski remembered a humorous incident at this camp:

"Mr. Kingsford was the man in charge of the Upper Peninsula [Michigan], all that woods and stuff; he was a regular woodsman, you couldn't fool him at night. He would start right through the woods around ten, ten-thirty, eleven o'clock at night. He'd walk out there through the woods; God knows where he was going; we didn't know. We slept two hundred feet from the game warden's house, but Mr. Kingsford had a spotlight, went up through the woods where there were some deer in an open field, and then he came right back to camp that night. In the morning after Mr. Kingsford got up, we had venison for breakfast!"

Following breakfast, August 7, the party spent some time walking

ABOVE: *Ford and Kingsford taking a siesta. (Detail of above photo.)*

ABOVE: *A detailed view of the tent layout and camp equipment on the Behan farm.*

ABOVE: *The camping party takes the ferry at Chazy Landing, New York, sailing past the islands in Lake Champlain, August 9. Left to right: Ford, Kingsford and Firestone.*

through the woods and exploring the surrounding country. Burroughs, quite naturally, took a great interest in the plant and bird life and gave his fellow campers some interesting bits of information from the vast memory bank accumulated during fifty years of study and observation in the field. About noon the camp caravan got under way, traveling slowly because of the poor condition of the roads. After passing through Tupper Lake, New York, the party stopped for lunch at a crossroads about eight miles beyond. There was a choice of two roads to the proposed campsite for that night near Lake Placid, New York. After some discussion the party had a friendly disagreement as to which route to take. Edison and Firestone opted for the dirt road, then got lost in the backwoods before arriving in Lake Placid two hours late.

Ford and Burroughs, and Harvey junior, led the caravan over a good macadam road, a direct route to their destination, which was four miles out of town; there they selected a beautiful campsite near the river.

Harvey met the late arrivals in Lake Placid and piloted them to camp. Following supper, some stories and yarns were exchanged around a blazing fire. Harvey junior had the good fortune to bump into some very close friends while in Lake Placid and he left camp to spend the night at John Barrett's place with his friends: Irving Harris, Hanford Twitchell, Alden Lofquist and Erd Harris.

Rain fell heavily on the morning of August 8, making it impossible to break camp until afternoon. Firestone took the opportunity to visit town and get a "city-shave" at the barbershop. The rest of the party stayed in camp for a postbreakfast nap. Harvey junior brought his father and the boys he had just visited back to camp; the boys were delighted to meet the celebrities. After they lunched on Chef Sato's renowned veal stew, the weather began to clear. As the party prepared for departure, an interruption came in the guise of several motion-picture photographers hoping to film some real-life camp scenes. The campers accepted their fate and allowed the cameramen to direct their motions and activities for the next quarter hour.

The telephone had preceded them in even the most out-of-the-way places, and the wires carried the news of their coming to every town and hamlet along their route. The result was that they were always being met by committees of leading citizens and escorted into town, wrapped in dust and glory, neither of which they enjoyed. Their cars were surrounded by people begging for speeches and autographs.

This was a tedious bore to Edison. He had not gone off "playing" to be met by bands and committees and to be importuned to burst into oratory. He liked friendliness, but he was restive under curiosity and adulation. Speeches he would not make. When he had to "do something" or look like a grouch, he would stand up in his automobile and smile and wave to the crowd. He would sign his name with that "umbrella" signature of his, but when the curious gathered, if he could get a newspaper and retire behind it, he did.

As a rule Edison was the center of attention. But there were times when the spotlight turned to Ford and Burroughs. In little villages Ford was a close second to Edison, or even surpassed him, as an object of public interest. The villagers were sometimes rather vague about Edison. His name had a sort of aura of glory, but they were not quite sure what it was all about. There was no uncertainty with regard to Ford. He was like a familiar, everyday object, a household word in the flesh.

Burroughs was less widely known. But when they came across people who were familiar with his writings, the spotlight moved, and the fine old interpreter of the fields and woods threw the rest of the party into the shadows.

About 2 p.m. the caravan got under way and headed for Plattsburgh, New York. After passing through the city, they made a return visit to the Behan farm, where a similar camp had been made on the 1916 trip. Mrs. Behan sent the campers some raspberry jam, apple pie and fresh milk, which contributed in no small way to their evening meal. Edison was in rare form, being in a more humorous mood than ever that evening, and told innumerable stories while everyone gathered around the campfire. The cheery warmth of the fire was appreciated as the night air grew ever colder; extra covers were needed for sleeping as the night was the coldest experienced during the trip.

When the campers started out on August 9, there was a consensus favoring a visit to Canada, with Montreal as a target. However, when they reached Chazy Landing, New York, they decided to take a ferry ride across Lake Champlain and then down through Vermont and to the White Mountains instead. So the whole caravan ferried across the lake. Everyone enjoyed the bracing air and the beautiful scenery before arriving in Burlington, Vermont, for lunch

ABOVE: *Edison demonstrates his technique for shaving—"Go up one side and down the other"—at Green Mountain camp on the Benson farm.*

BELOW: *An ideal shaded glen was selected for Green Mountain camp on the Benson farm, where the campers spent Sunday, August 9.*

ABOVE: *Ford conducts a geological experiment with, left, Edison and, right, Kingsford.*

at the Hotel Vermont.

Word of the party's arrival spread through the town, and by the time the campers were ready to take to the road again, a large crowd had gathered in front of the hotel. The caravan kept to the highway until 6 p.m. when a fine camping site on the Benson farm three miles from Stowe, Vermont, was located along the banks of a babbling brook. The tents were pitched in a grove of stately maples beside the cool stream. As darkness came on, the campfire was relighted and the entire party lounged about at peace with the world and with memories of a pleasant day.

August 10 dawned bright, but Burroughs declared himself a half-holiday. He said there was no necessity for early morning rising and stayed abed quite late. Ford and Firestone were up for an early breakfast, then took a long walk and inspected Benson's sugar camp. Although the weather was cloudy, their stay at Green Mountain camp was quite enjoyable. Lunch preceded their packing and getting on the road again in the midafternoon. A stop was made at St. Johnsbury, then it was on to the Elliott farm near Waterford, Vermont. There, belatedly, camp was set up, rain having started just as they were about to set up their tents. This day's run was rather short, just 50.6 miles.

Camp was set up in a little orchard alongside the road. The Elliott children, a boy and a girl, happened by and Ford struck up a conversation with them, asking where they lived, and so on. During this talk they said they had an Edison phonograph at home that did not work well, so their parents had sent it back to the Edison dealer. When it came back, it still squeaked. Ford responded, "You go tell your mother that we're going to fix that for you tonight." Later, after supper, Ford, Kingsford, Jimmy Smith and Harvey junior visited the

RIGHT: *Ford admires some Firestone advertising in the local newspaper with Edison and Firestone at Green Mountain camp, August 9.*

Elliott house. Ford took the phonograph, placed it upon the living room table and disassembled it. The problem was more than a quick oiling could remedy. A little ring on the end of the governor was the culprit. This was filed down, the phonograph put together and the squeak was gone. When Mrs. Elliott realized who the famous repairman was, she was astounded. Back at the camp that evening, Ford kidded Edison about people sending their phonograph down to the Edison dealer who could not fix it. Needless to say, this incident provided ammunition for future friendly ribbing sessions.

Practical jokes were frequent, as Loskowski was to recall:

"Mr. Ford liked to play tricks and jokes on people, and he played them quite often. I remember one where he had wooden tent stakes, and he had a fellow saw them up in little bits of square blocks, which he then put into the soup for dinner, so Mr. Firestone would bite on them. I'll never forget that!"

The next morning, August 11, the party got an early start and drove to Bretton Woods, New Hampshire, where telegrams and newspapers were awaiting various members. The drive through this section of the White Mountains was very beautiful and everyone appreciated the scenery and fine roads. The route took them through picturesque Crawford Notch and into North Conway. Burroughs's journal related his impressions of the trip:

"Not any drift boulders in Green and White Mountains, because the old ice-sheet plucked them from these mountains and dropped them over the landscape to the South; here they lie like a herd of slumbering elephants with their calves, sleeping the sleep of geologic ages. The view of the White Mountains was very impressive. They drove through Crawford Notch, down, down and down, over a superb road, through woods with these great rocky peaks shouldering the sky on each side. Simply stupendous!"

Firestone accompanied Burroughs, who decided to have a hot lunch at the Sunset Inn there. Ford and Edison, however, decided to stand by the usual roadside lunch and refused to depart from the camp routine. Good time was made in the afternoon with a rest stop called in Meredith, New Hampshire. Ford and Firestone noticed a towel factory in the town, and their manufacturer's curiosity aroused, they spent half an hour inspecting the plant.

ABOVE: *The local populace turned out to welcome the campers, who spent the night of August 11 at the Ideal Hotel in Tilton, New Hampshire.*

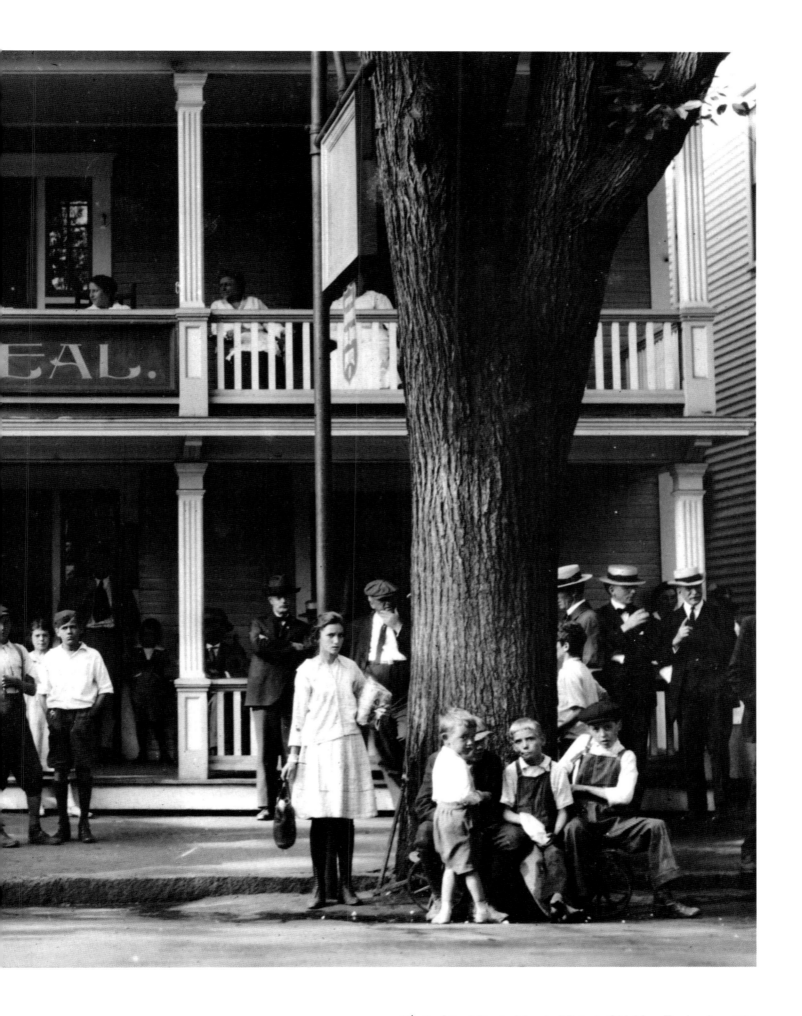

ABOVE: *A lunch stop at the Cheshire House in Keene, New Hampshire, attracted the usual crowd of well-wishers, August 12.*

ABOVE: *Burroughs catches up on the news of the day while Edison takes in the fresh air at Camp Hatfield, August 12.*

As was sometimes necessary, the trucks went on ahead, the crew planning to meet the campers at Lakeport, New Hampshire, near Lake Winnipesaukee. The campers missed them en route and did not realize it until they had reached Franklin, where a search for the lost commissary was undertaken, this task falling to Harvey junior. The long-distance line was employed and every police station between Franklin and Lakeport, a distance of some fifteen miles, was asked to be on the lookout. The Simplex was driven through to East Andover, New Hampshire, approximately seven miles past Franklin. To remain visible to the searching wayward ones, the famous four parked their cars in front of the Franklin Public Library on Central Street and lounged on a pleasantly shaded lawn under an eighty-year-old maple tree.

Unwittingly, they had chosen the most controversial plot of ground in town. The city council had voted to cut down the tree, but the library trustees had pleaded with the woodsman to spare it. The state supreme court had later decided that the city fathers were without authority to remove the tree. This happened after the whole community had become embroiled on one side or the other of the controversy. The *Manchester Union* and the *Franklin Journal Transcript*, two tree partisans, took editorial advantage of the "glorious time" that was enjoyed there by the campers. Harvey junior recorded the scene with his portable motion-picture camera.

The campers then retraced the four miles back to Tilton, where the supply train finally was located. It was then back to Franklin and a fortuitous hookup with the Simplex truck, which was returning from East Andover. After a conference on the situation, it was decided that the hour being late for selecting a campsite, the party would return to Tilton and register for the night at the Ideal Hotel. Fred Loskowski's comments on this incident are interesting:

"I remember once when we hit Franklin. They didn't want to camp that night. Mr. Firestone wanted a bath. He wouldn't take a bath like Mr. Ford would—he'd get out in the creek and take a bath. But Mr. Firestone—he'd stop at a hotel. It was about eight o'clock that night, so we pulled up at Franklin. The Boss hailed us and said, 'We're going to this hotel in Tilton tonight.' 'We're going to stay at a hotel!' I thought, 'Boy, that suits me just fine!' I was tired anyway. We had driven I don't know how many miles that day. I pulled ahead, and they pulled alongside the hotel. Jimmy Smith and I pulled in.

"Sato, with the cook car, didn't see them pull in. He kept right on going through Tilton. We waited, thinking he had gone two or three blocks, would turn around, then come back. By God, he didn't! Me and Jimmy Smith had to take the Cadillac, and we highballed after him. We caught him outside of the town—about twenty miles out—and turned him around. Boy! We spent our night that night chasing Sato! I'll never forget that! If we had a gun, we would have killed him that night, we were so mad at him. We were going to have a time in that town. We got back, put the cars away and went to sleep."

A crowd began to gather at the Ideal Hotel while the campers were finishing their evening meal, and within a half hour a large portion of the populace was in and around the hotel. The people were cordial and hospitable, the atmosphere congenial. Burroughs finally consented to give a short talk, which was received with enthusiasm. Edison and Ford then maneuvered so that Firestone was forced to mount the rostrum and tell the crowd how much the campers enjoyed their tour through New England. The Salvation Army had dispatched a squadron of fund-raisers into Tilton in order not to miss this golden opportunity, and Edison apparently decided that if he were going to serve as a public exhibit before a virtual mob, however friendly, the mob was going to pay for it. With a bound, he was off the veranda and down in the midst of the crowd, grabbing up a Salvation Army tambourine and passing through the assemblage, asking that they all contribute generously. When the tambourine began to overflow, Edison pressed a hat into service to hold the cascade of coins and bills.

Burroughs stayed the night with friends in Franklin, Dr. and Mrs. E. T. Drake. Mrs. Drake was a daughter of J. B. Aiken, who had been a chum of Burroughs in Florida years earlier.

After a good night's rest the whole party was up early the next morning, August 12, and Ford, Firestone and Edison dropped in on the Arthur S. Brown Manufacturing Company, which at the time held a fan belt contract with the Ford Motor Company. Burroughs visited the Drakes' cottage on Webster Lake prior to rejoining his traveling companions at Franklin.

The day's run took the campers through Newport with a stop at Keene, New Hampshire, for lunch. During the meal a large crowd gathered in front of the Cheshire Hotel to welcome the tourists. There was another delay for picture-taking, but the caravan finally drove off amid the cheers of the assemblage. Another delightful camping site was located among a grove of pines near a small waterfall. This proved to be the last evening meal in camp and chef Sato

ABOVE: *Sato attends to the campfire at Camp Hatfield, August 12.*

ABOVE: *Firestone looks over the tent row on the last night of camp at Hatfield, Connecticut, August 12.*

ABOVE: *A quiet stream provides an idyllic setting for the neatly lined up sleeping tents at the Hatfield, Massachusetts, camp.*

did himself proud.

All gathered around a roaring campfire after dark where Edison held court, proving himself in fine form again. His stories, comments and anecdotes were amusing as well as informative. One of his stories had as its subject a too-casual young woman who, when asked whether her latest offspring looked like its father, responded, "I'm not sure. I met the child's father at a masquerade ball!" Burroughs fell over backwards on his camp chair laughing; Ford didn't even crack a smile.

Firestone started to talk with Edison about rubber and its properties, and he was astounded by the breadth of knowledge the famed inventor had at hand. Firestone had been working with rubber for years, but Edison told him more than even the Firestone chemists knew. Edison had not given any great attention to rubber (except in connection with his talking machines), until he made some major discoveries later in his career. He was then as well informed on that subject as on any subject brought up with him.

While Edison and Burroughs remained behind next morning, August 13, to supervise the breaking of camp, Ford, Firestone and Kingsford, with Harvey junior, drove into Springfield, Massachusetts, to get their mail and do some shopping. An hour or so later the camp caravan made its appearance and the complete party again took to the open road. On arrival in Hartford, Connecticut, they lunched at the Hotel Bond. This was too near civilization for the campers, as evidenced by a battery of reporters who stood about the table, seeking news and views from the vagabond giants.

The next stop was Waterbury, Connecticut, where one section of the caravan waited for the other to catch up, while a public reception, larger than any that had gone before, began to burgeon. Here Burroughs, much to the regret of the other members of the party, felt that he must leave to keep an engagement he had made many weeks previously. After good-byes were said, the cars got under way immediately and headed for Danbury, Connecticut.

The camping party looked for a likely spot to set up their tents as the weather grew threatening, finally deciding to drive to Danbury and stay at the Hotel Greene overnight. The decision proved to be a wise one as it rained very hard that evening and the hotel proved much more comfortable than the open country would have been. In the evening Ford, Edison, Kingsford and the Firestones took a walk in the rain and later went to a movie.

The next morning, August 14, the weather was no better, so it was decided to end the 1919 camping trip. The campers headed for New York City, while the trucks and equipment were dispatched to Cleveland, Ohio, there to be loaded on the ferry for the lake voyage to Detroit. The Ford crew arrived at the Ford garage in Dearborn,

Michigan, about 9:30 a.m. Sunday.

Arriving in New York City about noon, the party lunched with Woodrow McKay at the Hotel Cumberland, and in the afternoon inspected the new Ford building on Broadway. Ford and Kingsford left by train that night for Detroit, and Firestone left for Akron, Ohio. Harvey junior remained in New York.

Summing up the trip, Burroughs wrote, "It often seemed to me that we were a luxuriously equipped expedition going forth to seek discomfort; after all, [that] is what the camper-out is unconsciously seeking. . .we react against our complex civilization and long to get back for a time to first principles."

This was to be Burroughs's last camping trip. Although he hosted a late fall cookout for his companions in November of the succeeding year, he was to pass away in March of 1921 at the venerable age of eighty-four. A second change occurred at the 1920 cookout, and on subsequent trips: the campers invited their wives to share their enjoyment of the great outdoors. The flavor, the fun and, indeed, the nature of future outings inevitably changed.

TOP: *John Burroughs bids good-bye to his fellow campers as he leaves the tour at Waterbury, Connecticut, August 13.*

ABOVE: *The Firestones met with employees of the Firestone Company branch in Hartford, Connecticut, as the camping trip of 1919 neared its end, August 13.*

CHRISTMAS HOST

1920

1920

ITINERARY

John Burroughs was Host in Rip Van Winkle Country

NOVEMBER 15 *The Fords, Edisons and Firestones met John Burroughs at the Yama Farms Inn, Napanoch, New York. They were joined there by Carl Akeley and Roy Chapman Andrews.*

NOVEMBER 16 *A tree-chopping contest between Ford and Burroughs. Hiking and other outdoor activities enjoyed by all.*

NOVEMBER 17 *From Yama Farms Inn the vacationers traveled to Burroughs's home, Riverby, in West Park, New York. Ford, Edison and Firestone spent a few hours with Burroughs at his nearby retreat, Slabsides. All guests were treated to a shish kebab cooked over an outdoor fireplace, then a buffet supper indoors.*

NOVEMBER 18 *The refreshing Catskill holiday came to a close.*

ABOVE: *The vacationers gather in the orchard at Yama Farms Inn on November 15, 1920. This is the first outing which included the wives. At left, Burroughs poses with Edison, Mina Edison, Clara Ford, Ford, Idabelle Firestone, Ursula Burroughs and Firestone.*

1920

JOHN BURROUGHS WAS HOST
"In Rip Van Winkle Country"

The year 1920 was the eighty-third year of John Burroughs's long, eventful life, and the sands of time were flowing relentlessly through the neck of his hourglass. Quite possibly he had a premonition that one final opportunity remained for another gathering of his beloved friends.

At this time the postwar economy was confronting the other campers with financial problems. Harvey Firestone had abruptly returned from abroad to address budgetary matters of his company. Henry Ford and Thomas Edison also were preoccupied with their respective empires. The approaching winter weather limited the options for a gathering, but after some correspondence and some earnest solicitation by Burroughs, it was finally agreed that he would host a holiday outing in the Catskill Mountains of New York State.

On November 15, 1920, everyone who was to participate in the holiday festivities met at Yama Farms Inn, a private resort at Napanoch, not far from New York City, for a few days of rest and recreation. The inn was owned by Walter Seaman, a generous friend of Burroughs, and a stay here, where one could enjoy the many comforts wealth could provide, was by invitation only. Two aspects of this outing were different from the previous encampments. First, this was a trip in which they slept indoors instead of in the open, and second, the wives—Mrs. Edison, Mrs. Ford and Mrs. Firestone—were invited, setting a precedent that was followed in each of the later camping trips.

John Burroughs had spent much of his time at this inn over the years. It was here in 1915 that he had received the sad news that his explorer-companion, John Muir(John O'Mountains), had passed away on December 24. His journal entry of 1915 recorded his feelings:

"An event I have been expecting for more than a year—a unique character—greater as a talker than a writer—he loved personal combat and shone at it—he hated writing and composed with difficulty, though his books have charm of style, but his talk

ABOVE: *"Go," shouts Edison to the contestants in a tree chopping contest as referee Firestone looks on approvingly, November 16.*

came easily and showed him at his best, I shall greatly miss him."

Two world-famous explorers, Carl Akeley and Roy Chapman Andrews, joined the party at the inn, and around the big wood fireplace at night Akeley told of his adventures in Africa, while Andrews described some of his exploits in archaeological research. Both men were resting up for a new venture into the wild countries of the world.

The crisp autumn air of the Catskills, with occasional flurries of snow, made walking along the mountain roads a delight for all members of the party. Walking about was the chief daytime recreation. Ford, when he was out-of-doors, was just like a boy; he wanted to have footraces, to climb trees or to do anything a boy might do. He customarily ate very little and always kept himself in first-class physical condition. Walking, skating and dancing were of great interest to him, but he demonstrated no interest at all in games

such as golf.

A tree-chopping contest, which proved to be the highlight of the day, pitted Ford against Burroughs. Two saplings were selected in the woods near the inn. Edison acted as timekeeper and Firestone was referee. At a signal from Firestone the two men swung their axes. Burroughs was judged the winner, with several seconds to spare, to the applause of the gallery of wives and other visitors. Edison was the first to congratulate the victor and told Burroughs, "These youngsters aren't in our class at all." He consoled Ford with the assurance he had many years before him in which to become proficient in the lumber craft. Exuberant over his victory, Burroughs offered to take on anyone in a tree-climbing contest, but could find no takers.

The evening of November 16 was spent at the inn, with a big log burning in the fireplace and everyone joining in lively discussions on various topics, spiced with some humorous and interesting tales.

Burroughs told stories about life on his remote farm in the early part of the century. He convulsed the audience when he told how he had drudged long hours on the treadmill of the one-dog-power butter churn when Old Cuff, the farm dog whose job it was to provide power, went AWOL.

From Yama Farms Inn, the vacationers went by automobile the next day, November 17, to Burroughs's home, Riverby, in West Park, New York, a little more than an hour away.

Burroughs had developed Riverby over a period of years, starting with the purchase of nine acres along the banks of the Hudson River in 1873. He added to this acreage in later years, so that the estate came in time to comprise twenty acres. Although he and Mrs. Burroughs were to dwell forty-seven years in this river abode, he continued to speak of Woodchuck Lodge, in Roxbury, New York, as home.

He had labored for three days creating a pasteboard model for the stone house, which took shape as he oversaw the stonemason's

ABOVE: *This setting (November, 1920) proved to be the last occasion when the travelers would pose together. Their bond was broken when Burroughs passed away in March, 1921.*

RIGHT: *Ford's axe finds its mark.*

work (not too smooth, not too much mortar showing), and he climbed the hills and helped fell trees for the planing mill. He made trips to his native Catskill haunts for butternut, cherry, curly maple and ash, which a year later were viewed as casings, baseboard and paneling in his home.

By 1902 Burroughs's son, Julian, had constructed a cottage nearby. He named it Lovecote because he had brought his wife to it as a bride. With their children they were to reside there for twelve years. In 1914 Burroughs's assistant, Dr. Clara Barrus, and her two "birdlings" (children) occupied the cottage, which they renamed the Nest. Mr. and Mrs. John Burroughs were living nearby at Riverby when, Dr. Barrus recalled, by June 1, "John O' Birds and Mrs. John O' Birds began to dine and sup with us; and with the two birdlings within, and the wrens in their boxes on the veranda post, robins in the rosebushes, catbirds in the lilacs, wood thrushes in the maples, orioles in the elms, and swifts in the chimney, the 'Nest' was a nest indeed!"

Wednesday afternoon Ford, Edison and Firestone joined Burroughs for a quiet interlude at his rugged mountain cabin,

Slabsides, which served as a retreat a little less than a two-mile hike from Riverby.

Julian Burroughs described his father's fascination with the development of Slabsides in *The Slabsides Book*, published in 1931:

"Owning a piece of the beloved woods where he had tramped and studied nature so often, Father began to 'take root' as he expressed it. He soon wanted a cabin, a place truly his own, a retreat where he could do exactly as he wished, a means of escape from the tyranny of the housework at Riverby. This 'tyranny,' of which he so often spoke, was wholly impersonal. The work 'had to be done.' The routine of the house was almost military; not for a moment did Mother realize that she alone was responsible for this. To her it was all governed by some higher law, something akin to a religion for which she was but the instrument. She never understood that this

was irksome to Father, that he should want a place to 'invite his soul,' as he expressed it, a place where nothing just 'had to be done' at once, where relaxation and repose were of vastly more importance than housework.

"There were other reasons: at Slabsides, Father could invite whomever he wished, at any time, without upsetting any household routine. Truly, at Slabsides he found his heart's desire, while personages such as John Muir, Walt Whitman, Henry Ford, Robert Underwood Johnson and President Theodore Roosevelt would pay

LEFT: *The contestants at the finish.*

ABOVE: *Burroughs, the winner at the finish, receives congratulations from Edison.*

136   JOHN BURROUGHS WAS HOST *In Rip Van Winkle Country*

him a visit." Somewhat later, Elizabeth Burroughs Kelley, John Burroughs's granddaughter, penned the following historical anecdote relating to Slabsides:

"Of all the celebrities who came to Slabsides it was Theodore Roosevelt who caused the most excitement in the neighborhood since he was at the time the President of the United States and Presidents did not get about then as they do now. On July 10 in 1903 the President and Mrs. Roosevelt came up the Hudson on the Presidential yacht [Sylph] and my grandfather and my father [Julian] were on the West Park dock to meet them when they came ashore. They were in good spirits and decided to take the walk of well over a mile and a half to the cabin, which was a steeper climb. 'You should

have seen Theodore climb the hill!' exclaimed Burroughs. 'He clenched his fists and gritted his teeth and came up like a race-horse! However, Mrs. Roosevelt didn't seem to make the slightest effort, and yet she got to the top as soon as he did!'

"Though it was intensely hot the President seemed quite unconscious of it, listening eagerly for every bird note or song as they walked along the dusty road to the woods, talking now on natural history, now on politics, the Post Office scandal, incidents of his Western tour, a sketch of some European monarch, literary criticism—all with unbounded vigor and clearness.

"At ten o'clock John Burroughs started the fire in the fireplace to broil two chickens and bake the potatoes and onions. Mrs. Roosevelt helped shell the peas from the muck garden and these were cooked over the little oil stove. On the menu were lettuce and celery also from the garden and they had sweet cider and spring water to drink. Mrs. Burroughs topped it all off with homemade cherry pie, and after the group returned approximately the mile and a half to Riverby, she served homemade ice cream.

"As the Roosevelts had to leave West Park in time to reach Hell's Gate in New York before dark they could not linger very long but they did sit for a while in the summerhouse where they had a fine view of the Vanderbilts' palatial home across the river. There was time also to see the house my father built [Lovecote] and the President was much impressed by it. 'Edie,' he called to Mrs. Roosevelt, 'you must see this. It is truly American.' The Vanderbilts, so my father learned later, were at the time looking through their glasses at the yacht anchored in front of them for—surprise!—it flew the President's flag!"

Upon returning to Riverby from Slabsides with the group, Burroughs, endowed as he was with the love of nature, gave a "cannibal steak" party for the vacationers on this late fall afternoon in 1920. All the guests converged on an open space near the woods,

ABOVE LEFT: *This study in Slabsides provided Burroughs with the tranquil environment he needed for his nature writings.*

ABOVE: *The cheery hearth of Slabsides.*

ABOVE: *Slabsides, the rustic mountain retreat where Burroughs spent many happy hours communing with nature.*

ABOVE: *Burroughs's pasteboard model of his house at Riverby.*

ABOVE: *Burroughs starts the cooking fire for the brigand steaks. Snowflakes from sporadic snow showers that afternoon remain on the ground.*

ABOVE: *Julian Burroughs's house, Lovecote, later known as the Nest, near Riverby, West Park, New York.*

where everyone helped to start a cooking fire amidst sporadic snow. Burroughs would select a straight, green limb and sharpen its end, then cut a big brigand steak into pieces and slip them over the wooden skewer with bits of bacon and little green onions between the slices, then hand it to a guest who would broil it over the glowing coals of the fire. A picnic at Tyrell Lake, New York, in May of 1916 was the occasion when the Reverend Franklin D. Elmer, pastor of the First Baptist Church of Poughkeepsie, instructed Burroughs in the fine art of preparing a brigand steak shish kebab.

With the open fireplace cooking completed, everyone was treated to a tasty buffet supper inside Lovecote. The crisp chill in the air had sharpened appetites and many complements testified to the delicious fare.

That evening was spent very comfortably in the warm indoors at Riverby, where congeniality prevailed, stories abounded and the elements for future reflections were firmly established. The next day, November 18, the party broke up, each guest leaving for home refreshed and with memories of an excellent holiday.

Burroughs's premonition, if such there was, was to become reality in a few short months, so this was the last time the foursome would rendezvous with the express intention of discovering God's truth in nature.

A nostalgic reflection on Burroughs's adventure-packed life reveals that even though he was a world traveler, one who was hosted by Presidents of the United States, a nature writer of the first

water, his heart always remained in the tiny village of Roxbury, his birthplace and the locale of his rustic cottage, Woodchuck Lodge.

Burroughs and Ford were at odds over Ford's new-fangled contraption, the automobile. Burroughs's position was that God had divined man to walk. Ford sought Burroughs's acquaintance, and Burroughs's journal of 1913 recorded the event:

"In Detroit with Mr. Ford and Mr. Glen Buck. Have a fine time. Mr. Ford pleased with me and I with him. His interest in birds is keen, and his knowledge considerable. A loveable man. The Ford plant covers over 49 acres. The cars grow before your eyes, and

TOP: *After all his world travels Burroughs still considered Woodchuck Lodge his "home".*

ABOVE: *Ford pays a visit to Burroughs at Woodchuck Lodge in 1915. They look over the valley of Roxbury in the Catskill Mountains of New York.*

LEFT: *The fire is nicely underway as Ford and Burroughs await hot coals with which to cook the shish kebab, November 17.*

RIGHT: *The guests gather around as Burroughs demonstrates the art of preparing brigand steak.*

ABOVE: *Burroughs in his cantankerous Model T touring car that was a gift from his fellow camper and bird lore enthusiast, Ford. Woodchuck Lodge, his favorite place, is just "up the road a piece."*

every day a thousand of them issue from the rear."

Later, on June 7, he wrote further:

"We spent the day at Mr. Ford's farm—where he has an electric launch on a small river, and a big bungalow in the woods—I like Mr. Ford and his wife much—his interest in birds makes him forget everything else for the moment. He wants to give me more things— among them a closed car for winter use; but I told Buck to head him off." Notwithstanding this reticence, Ford presented Burroughs with a brand-new 1913 Model T touring car, this largesse probably to lessen the grand old man's steely reluctance to accept any progress that involved the iron contraption. The auto was shipped express to West Park, and Buck arrived from Detroit to instruct Burroughs in its operation.

On June 28 Julian drove his father on their first ride from West Park to Roxbury. The day that Julian was to leave Woodchuck Lodge to return by train to West Park, Burroughs's journal notes the following experience with the car:

"Came home and ran it into the locust tree just inside our gates— the little beast sprang for that tree like a squirrel. How ready it is to take to a ditch, or a tree or a fence. In driving the car in the old barn I get rattled and let it run wild; it bursts through the side of the barn like an explosion. There is a great splintering and rattling of boards and timbers, and the car stops with its forward axle hanging out over a drop of 15 feet. As the wheels went out, the car dropped on its flywheel, and that saved me. The wheel caught on less than a foot from the edge; had it not, it would have landed at the foot of a steep hill, and I should have landed on the other side of Jordan. The top of the radiator is badly crumpled, otherwise the car is unhurt. I am terribly humiliated and, later, scared by my narrow escape."

Subsequently, one day while Ford was visiting Burroughs at Woodchuck Lodge, Burroughs chanced to mention that if he owned the farm he would make a few changes. Ford went to the owner, Burroughs's nephew, John C., asked whether he would sell and at

Burrough-
Form 200

Akron, O., Mar. 29, 1921.

T.A.Edison:

Strain on Mr. Burroughs on his trip to California was more than he could endure and he died in Buffalo this morning. Hope our Camping party can arrange to attend his funeral.

H. S. FIRESTONE

Let me know where & when funeral takes place

what price, wrote out a check on the spot and handed it to him. Now the naturalist owned his birthplace, but he was to die a short time later, with the farm passing to his son, Julian. Again Ford wrote out a check and acquired both the farm and Woodchuck Lodge in his own name. He assisted in renovating and restoring the place to its natural beauty while an active member of the John Burroughs Memorial Association.

Woodchuck Lodge stands today much as Burroughs left it—rustic furniture, which he made himself, his pictures, and the last words he was to pen in Roxbury: "Oct. 26, 1920, leave here today." He penciled them on the siding of the porch as he left his home, which was closest to his heart, for the last time.

Burroughs spent the winter traveling and visiting in California, where illness put him in the hospital for a lengthy stay. His condition had deteriorated when they placed him in a berth aboard the train for the springtime return to his beloved Catskill Mountains. Death came peacefully, at Buffalo, a few miles from his final destination of West Park, on March 29, 1921, his eighty-fourth natal year.

While the nation mourned, Ford, Edison and Firestone joined a few friends who had gathered at The Nest at Riverby on April 2 for brief services; on April 3, his eighty-fourth birthday, his body was laid to rest by his Boyhood Rock, on the farm where he was born near Roxbury.

ABOVE: *Firestone notifies Edison of the loss of their beloved friend, John Burroughs.*

BELOW: *Edison and Burroughs as they enjoy the view at Ford Rock at Woodchuck Lodge in 1916.*

HARDING CAMP

1921

1921
ITINERARY

The President Harding Camp, in the Maryland Mountains

JULY 21   *Mr. and Mrs. Henry Ford sailed on the yacht Sialia from Detroit, Michigan, to Cleveland, Ohio, to meet Mr. and Mrs. Harvey Firestone, Sr. Group joined at Columbiana, Ohio, by Mr. amd Mrs. Harvey Firestone, Jr., and Russell Firestone. Party completed by Mr. and Mrs. Edsel Ford. Dinner served by Women's Missionary Society of the Grace Reformed church, then group motored to Bedford Springs, Pennsylvania. Stayed overnight at hotel.*

JULY 22   *Fords and Firestones traveled to Hagerstown, Maryland, met Mr. and Mrs. Thomas Edison and Bishop and Mrs. William Anderson. Crew set up camp at Pecktonville, Maryland.*

JULY 23   *President Warren G. Harding and his secretary, George B. Christian, Jr., greeted by campers at Funkstown, Maryland, and escorted to the campsite. Men took an afternoon ride on Firestone's saddle horses.*

JULY 24   *Another horse ride taken after breakfast. Bishop Anderson conducted church services in a wood chapel. President Harding left camp for return to Washington, D.C.*

JULY 25   *Camped on at Pecktonville. Mr. and Mrs. Edsel Ford left for home.*

JULY 26   *Remained at Pecktonville.*

JULY 27   *Firestone horses shipped to Akron, Ohio. Broke camp, motored through Kaisers Ridge, Maryland, lunched at Deer Park. Set up camp at Swallow Falls, Maryland.*

JULY 28   *Spent a leisurely day at the Swallow Falls camp. Borrowed ponies from neighboring campers.*

JULY 29   *Remained at Swallow Falls, relaxed and enjoyed surrounding nature.*

JULY 30   *Heavy rainstorms and impassable roads forced the party to remain in camp at Swallow Falls.*

JULY 31   *Broke camp, then moved out to Elkins, West Virginia. Stayed at a hotel as camp equipment did not arrive.*

AUGUST 1   *Mr. and Mrs. Harvey Firestone, Jr., and Russell Firestone left camp for Washington, D.C. Camped at Cheat River near Elkins. Ford and Firestone were requested to return to their business enterprises.*

AUGUST 2   *Campers departed Elkins to Fairmont (noon). Rained at Wheeling, West Virginia, causing reroute through Morgantown to Uniontown, Pennsylvania, and a stop at the Summit Hotel.*

AUGUST 3   *Left Uniontown for Pittsburgh, where Edisons and Fords continued on to their respective homes.*

ABOVE: *President Warren G. Harding joins the party for a camping weekend at Camp Harding, July 23. The presidential flag on the chief executive's automobile waves proudly. Welcoming the President are, left to right, Edsel Ford, Russell Firestone, Harvey Firestone, President Harding, Mrs. William Anderson, Bishop William Anderson, presidential secretary George Christian, Jr., and Mrs. Thomas Edison.*

1921

THE PRESIDENT HARDING CAMP

"In the Maryland Mountains."

In the winter of 1921 and the ensuing spring, Henry Ford and Thomas Edison discussed plans for a camping trip the following summer. It was proposed that for the first time these veteran campers take along their wives. The pros and cons were discussed on several occasions, and the wives were consulted. Ford and Firestone thought it a worthy innovation, but Edison doubted its practicability, principally because he thought the women might not appreciate the primitiveness of camp conditions or take pleasure in roaming over the unbeaten track, which was one of Edison's greatest joys on these trips.

The decision having finally been made to include the women, Firestone, on one of his trips to Washington–accompanied by Bishop William F. Anderson of Ohio–made a call at the White House to propose a camping trip to President Warren G. Harding. Firestone had known the President for a long time; in fact, they had met when Harding was lieutenant governor of Ohio. The President accepted gladly, with the caveat that his presence depended upon affairs of state and the request that the camping be done somewhere within a reasonable driving distance from Washington, D.C.

In the latter part of June 1921, Firestone and Bishop Anderson made a second call at the White House and were advised definitely that the President and Mrs. Harding would be able to join the camping trip, which was scheduled for late July. Firestone was again in Washington on July 16 and had a conference with President Harding and the Secret Service staff at the White House as to arrangements for the President's attendants. Plans for the trip were outlined in detail to the Secret Service staff and the probable locations of the camps given, so that all necessary precautions could be taken.

During the week of July 17, however, Mrs. Harding was taken ill, so the President's plans to leave with her for the camp on July 22 had to be changed. Instead, the President remained at Mrs. Harding's bedside Friday evening until assured that her condition posed no danger and that he could join the camping party the next day.

ABOVE: *The crew takes a breather while setting up camp at Pecktonville, Maryland, on July 23. Harold Sato, the Japanese cook, is standing. Seated, are left to right, Harry Linden, Firestone horse groomer, Fred Loskowski, Jimmy Smith and Chef Fisher.*

BELOW: *President Harding immediately doffed his coat and got busy with the axe at the camp woodpile, July 23.*

Meanwhile, the Firestones and Fords were already on the way to the camp. The Fords sailed aboard their private yacht, the *Sialia*, from Detroit to Cleveland, Ohio, joining the Firestones there. This group reached the Firestone homestead near Columbiana, Ohio, by 12:30 p.m. on July 21. The Firestones were accompanied by their son Harvey junior and his bride of a few weeks, Elizabeth Parke Firestone, and another son, Russell. The Fords were accompanied by their son Edsel and his wife, Eleanor Clay Ford, who had arrived about noon.

The Firestone homestead had been in the family for more than 130 years, and the old brick house, built in 1828 by Harvey's great-grandfather, was a landmark in that section of the country. (The homestead has now been moved to Greenfield Village, Dearborn, Michigan.) The Women's Missionary Society of the Grace Reformed Church had prepared dinner for them, and with typical country hospitality had also prepared cooked foods for the trip east in a refrigerated truck. A large refrigerator truck was loaded with farm produce from the Firestone farms, including chickens and various meats and vegetables. Firestone's Aunt Nannie Lower baked some goodies for the campers. After returning to the White House, President Harding penned a lovely letter telling her how much he had appreciated and enjoyed her chickens, cookies and cakes.

After their meal, about 3 p.m., the party left the farm accompanied by maids, helpers and attendants, and headed for Bedford Springs, Pennsylvania, which they reached by nightfall, completing the first lap on their journey.

Meanwhile, Mr. Hamilton and Fred Loskowski, Ford employees, stayed in Akron, Ohio, to await delivery of more equipment

July 21. A new Reo truck was still being serviced at that time. Loskowski later recalled:

"They finished the truck about 4 p.m. We loaded it and were on our way at five o'clock. We got to Hagerstown, Maryland, not that night, but the following night or next morning, somewhere around there. We kept right on driving. We stopped over for about three hours' sleep. One town there, a Ford dealer told us what hotel to go to. Me and Hamilton went in there, and then we batted through, because the folks were going to be there."

On the morning of July 22, the Ford-Firestone contingent reached Hagerstown and were joined by Mr. and Mrs. Edison, who arrived a few hours later from West Orange, New Jersey, with a portable radio outfit for use in camp, and by Bishop and Mrs. Anderson, who had come from Washington, D.C. The same day the entire party took lunch at a hotel in town.

After lunch the group forced its way through the crowds in the lobby of the hotel and in the street, got into their cars and drove to the camp, which was located about two miles north of the state road, running between Hancock and Hagerstown, and about six miles east of Hancock, near a small settlement called Pecktonville. It was one of those secluded spots that abound in that section of the country, but remain hidden from the harried motorist who bounds over the macadam just minutes away. Few, except natives of Washington County, had seen it since the 1860s, when Union and Confederate forces operated back and forth across the Potomac in bloody conflicts. A few miles west of Fairview Mountain, which offers one of the most charming prospects to be found in Maryland—the Potomac revealing itself in half a dozen places and

ABOVE: *A detailed view of the Camp Harding layout at Pecktonville, Maryland.*

the valley stretched out to the south beyond the river—a country road branches to the north, climbing a steep hill. Ten minutes' travel and the broad roadway is forgotten. This is the back country. Then the road dips, turns and loses itself in a little valley that lies on both sides of Licking Creek. There, a mile or so from where Licking Creek empties into the Potomac, was the site of the camp. It is called the Island, because a little stream breaks away from Licking Creek, wanders through the meadow a quarter of a mile, and then rejoins the creek.

Most of the camp equipment had arrived at this location on July 22. The Reo truck with the camping equipment was driven by Loskowski; Harold Sato drove the Lincoln, which served as the cook car; and Hamilton, Mrs. Ford's chauffeur, drove the big White truck. Firestone brought along George Ebbing to photograph the camping activites. Ford brought a specially equipped truck, driven by Floyd Rappot, which had a camp stove and special food compartments, enabling the party to make a hot meal along the wayside if desired. Ford also had special electrical equipment, in addition to

RIGHT: *The camp commissary setup with chefs Fisher, left, and Herman, right, preparing some tasty fare for the presidential campers, July 23.*

Edison's, for lighting the camp at night. He supervised the unloading and erection of tents, with canvas floors and fifty cots with white sheets and warm blankets, as well as electric lights for the sleeping quarters. The truckload of food from the Firestone farm had also arrived, including two refrigerators with several hundred pounds of meat, butter, eggs, milk, melons and one hundred dressed chickens. The rear of the truck folded down into a table. There were easy chairs and steamer chairs, magazines and newspapers. Two chefs, Herman and Fisher, white caps and all, and Sato, the Japanese chef and butler in a white jacket, were on hand, and so was a laboratory expert from the Ford Motor Company. A specially padded motor truck had carried six fine blooded horses to camp, including Harbel, which belonged to Firestone.

Mrs. Ford noticed a shortage of blankets and pillows, so she sent Loskowski and a helper into Hagerstown, where they bought all the needed bedding they could find. Preparations were made to accommodate some eighty persons, half of whom were attached to President Harding's staff. Loskowski recalled that it looked like a

ABOVE: *The campers join President Harding for an informal picture before start of morning church services in the grove, July 24.*

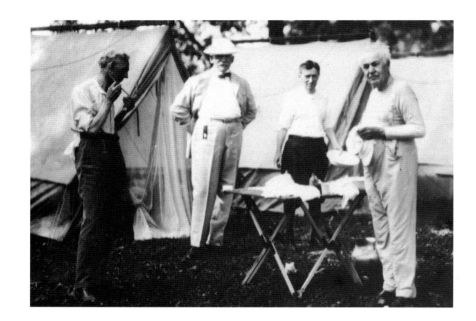

RIGHT: *Bishop Anderson, arms folded behind him, watches as the campers wash and shave. Left to right: Ford, Firestone, Edison.*

RIGHT: *Bishop Anderson conducts Sunday morning services for the President and the rest of the camping party, July 24.*

RIGHT: *Bishop Anderson, left foreground, passes the potatoes to President Harding, right background, using the Lazy Susan turntable that proved to be a hit with the campers at Camp Harding, July 24.*

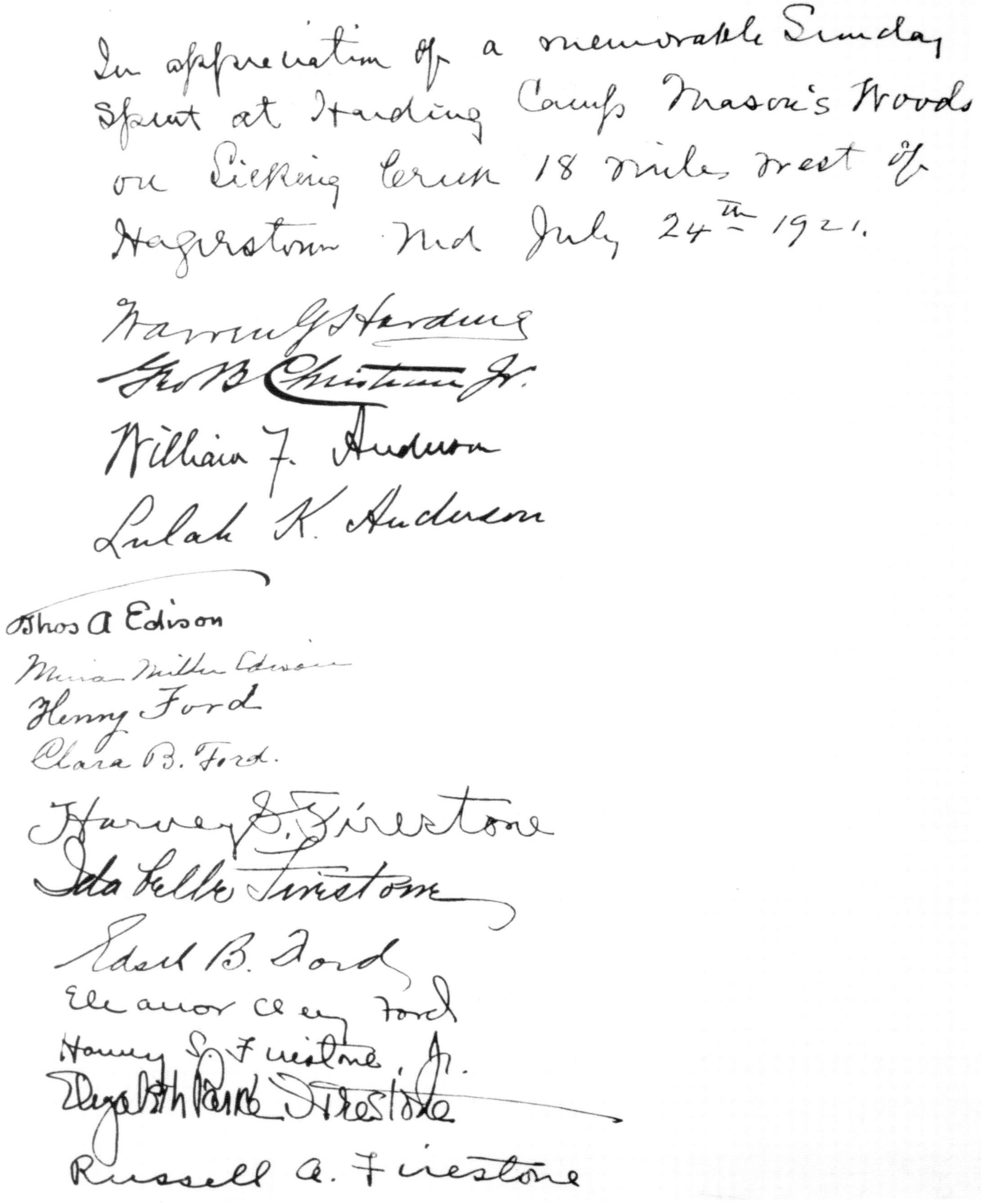

In appreciation of a memorable Sunday
spent at Harding Camp Mason's Woods
on Licking Creek 18 miles west of
Hagerstown Md July 24th 1921.

Warren G Harding
Geo B Christian Jr.
William J. Anderson
Lulah K. Anderson

Thos A Edison
Mina Miller Edison
Henry Ford
Clara B. Ford.

Harvey S. Firestone
Ida Belle Firestone
Edsel B. Ford
Eleanor Clay Ford
Harvey S. Firestone Jr.
Elizabeth Parke Firestone
Russell A. Firestone

ABOVE: *President Harding pens a note of appreciation for his enjoyable camping experience with his famous companions as the campers affix their respective signatures in approval.*

ABOVE: *Edison signs Harding's thank you note with his famous umbrella signature, July 24.*

BELOW: *Ford looks over the camp register as Russell Firestone and Edsel Ford await their turn.*

"young circus," but that a beautiful time was had by all on this camping trip. When everything was set up, the crew entertained itself by shooting craps and playing cards.

Edison, as he surveyed the campsite and all its equipment, was a bit skeptical about the success of this year's tour. It was a bit too elaborate for him and it seemed too comfortable. It had always been Edison's boast that on these trips the campers got very close to nature. He always chose the route and liked to take unbeaten trails and roads with little or no traffic. As Edison expressed his doubts about the enlarged layout at the campgrounds, Ford and Firestone pointed out that he himself had added to the conveniences of the camp by bringing special battery equipment for the lights, and a radio, which in those days was not a very common instrument.

While Ford was occupied with camp logistics, Edison and Firestone explored the site thoroughly and wandered about the surrounding woodland. In the early evening a campfire was built and the party gathered around it for an evening of congenial conversation. All retired rather early, however, in anticipation of the arrival of President Harding the following day.

The President left the White House for the camp about 9:30 a.m. on July 23, accompanied by his secretary, George B. Christian, Jr., and his wife, and the usual quota of Secret Service agents. Permission was granted to the ten regular White House newspaper correspondents, and nine newsreel photographers, to stay at the camp during the President's visit, as the gathering of these four men was looked upon in the daily press at the time as a highly newsworthy event.

Meantime, the campers left the camp about 10 a.m. and drove through Hagerstown, Maryland, on Route 40 to meet President Harding and escort him to the camp. This route at the time was

called the National Pike—The Road That Made the Nation—and it took them to the appointed meetingplace at Funkstown, Maryland, a quaint rural village steeped in Civil War lore. It was here, immediately following the Battle of Gettysburg, that the Union and Confederate forces had reengaged.

The President drove at a speedy pace from the White House, averaging more than fifty miles an hour, taxing the ability of his Secret Service agents and the newspapermen to keep up with him. He arrived at Funkstown just a few minutes after the camping party, meeting them just outside the village at the edge of the road.

THE BATTLE OF FUNKSTOWN

On Friday morning, July 10, 1863, General J. E. B. Stuart met General John Buford at Funkstown as General Robert E. Lee was drawing a battle line, nine miles long, near Williamsport, Maryland. Lee was unable to retreat across the Potomac River, its waters running extremely high at the time.

Sunup on Saturday morning revealed the opposing forces, and the ensuing battle swept across the northeast section of the town, as shells and shot struck many houses. Heavy cannon fire forced many townspeople to spend the day in their cellars. Casualties were very high, and the wounded were brought into Mrs. Chaney's large dwelling (today a fine antique shop), which had been commandeered for a field hospital.

Soldiers, many of whom died from their wounds, lay upon the floors in rows. In the evening, Mr. Chaney's Negro slaves sang spirituals for the dying. The surgeons had placed a table under some trees and there they amputated arms and legs, while townspeople administered to the wounded. There were 479 casualties—men either killed or wounded—196 Union and 283 Confederate soldiers. The Battle of Funkstown ended when the swollen waters of the Potomac receded sufficiently to allow General Lee to cross on the night of July 13, 1863.

RIGHT: *The Fords, father and son, spend a pensive moment together. Here, left to right, Henry and Edsel stand by one of the Model T Fords that were brought to the Harding Camp at Mason's Woods, July 23.*

BELOW: *Edsel Ford starts up the player piano for his father during a fun time on the evening of July 23, at Camp Harding, Maryland.*

President Harding got out of his car and Edison and Ford, who had never met the President, were introduced to him. He then got into the campers' car, sitting on the back seat with Edison, while Ford and Firestone sat on the folding jump seats. In front with the chauffeur a Secret Service agent occupied Edison's usual seat. The rest of the Secret Service detail followed in the President's car; still other detectives had been sent on ahead to the campsite.

President Harding had a charming manner and the rare ability to make friends easily. He pulled out some cigars and offered one to Edison. "No, thank you," answered Edison. "I don't smoke, I chew." Edison did smoke a great deal, but he was not going to take a cigar just because the President of the United States offered him one. Edison did not take to everyone at once; with no pretensions, he never set himself up as a hail-fellow-well-met. "I think I can accommodate you," answered the President, and with that he pulled a big plug of chewing tobacco out of his hip pocket. Edison thereupon grinned and took a big chew as he announced, "Harding is all right. Any man who chews tobacco is all right!"

As they passed through Hagerstown on the way to camp, they were greeted by large crowds which had assembled to see the party. It was nearly 1 p.m. when they rolled into the camp. The President was enthusiastic about the location. The noon meal was almost ready, but within ten minutes of greeting the members of the party who had remained in camp, the President had his coat off and was busy at the woodpile. Ford, who claimed to be no mean wood chopper himself, took the axe from the President when he stopped for a rest, and set to work himself. President Harding watched Ford with a critical eye for a few minutes, and then joined the camp circle nearby, where he obliged the cameramen by drinking water out of a long-handled dipper and chatting with each of the celebrities in turn. Loskowski, in his later years of retirement from the Ford Motor Company, was to remember the camp security:

"The Secret Service men were all over; you didn't know where they were and you didn't know who they were. We didn't pay much attention to them. The local press and people were pretty good about leaving the gang alone. Of course, the Secret Service men took care of everything like that. I told those fellows, 'You know your outfit, as long as they don't bother our outfit, it'll be all right.' They said, 'We will watch them. We know who is supposed to come in and who is not.' They were nice about it, and we had a wonderful stay there. Everybody had a good time."

When luncheon was announced, the whole party entered the dining tent, a specially built one designed by Ford. President Harding, like the rest of the men, was coatless as he sat down at the table between Mrs. Ford and Mrs. Firestone. The President was particularly intrigued with the table. It was a very large, round Lazy

ABOVE: *A camp scene where Edison warmed up to President Harding after Edison had received a chew of tobacco from the chief executive on the way to camp, July 23.*

ABOVE: *President Harding reviews Firestone's saddle horses prior to an afternoon ride into the surrounding countryside. Left to right: Russell Firestone, Harvey Firestone, Jr., his wife Eleanor, George Christian, Jr., presidential secretary, Harvey Firestone, Sr., and the President, July 23.*

BELOW: *Dorothy Murray, a young girl living nearby, presents a bouquet of wild flowers to President Harding as he pauses a moment during the ride, July 23.*

Susan table, comfortably seating every member of the party. But its unique feature was a turntable top in the center—a few inches above the dining table top—which provided space for all the various dishes and which, with an easy turn, could send them around to anyone desiring any particular food. When the President asked Mr. Firestone to pass the pepper, Firestone obliged by spinning the revolving center so that the section containing the pepper stopped just in front of the President.

The luncheon menu consisted of broiled lamb chops, grilled ham, boiled potatoes, corn on the cob, hot biscuits, watermelon and coffee. The conversation at this first meal in the camp was on general topics, the President inquiring about Edison's health and talking a bit with every member of the group. When lunch was over the campers picked up their chairs and retired under a canopy of elms and sycamores to chat. Turning to Edison, the President asked him what he did for recreation. "Oh, I eat and think," was Edison's reply. "Ever take up golf?" inquired the President. "No, I am not old enough," was the inventor's answer.

Shortly thereafter, Edison buried himself in a paper; Firestone wandered around the camp; President Harding retired to his tent for an afternoon nap; and Ford began to chop wood for the campfire. After a while Edison took a pillow, and moving over beneath one of the large elm trees, lay down on the ground for his nap.

Firestone and Ford sauntered down to the cook's tent and were beseeched by news cameramen to put on a wood-chopping contest. Firestone started first, but when he saw the apprehension which his chopping caused among the spectators, he quit after a few blows on the fence rail. Ford took up the axe and cut enough firewood for the

evening meal.

Ford was then asked to crank one of his own make of cars. He replied that all of the Fords in camp had self-starters. But when they asked him to crank one anyway, he stepped to the front of one of the Model T's and gave an exhibition with his usual good humor. The crowd applauded as he drove about the camp.

During these afternoon activities the women of the party sat around chatting and knitting. After an hour's rest, President Harding emerged from his tent, and looking very much refreshed, announced that he was ready for the next activity on the camp's program. He grabbed up the axe and returned to the woodpile, where he resumed chopping for a while. Afterward he and Firestone wandered down to the edge of Licking Creek and viewed the cool water while the President reminisced about swimming holes that he had known in his youth.

ABOVE: *The campers participate in an afternoon trot down a country road near Pecktonville, Maryland, July 23. Left to right: the President, Harvey Firestone, Jr., George Christian, Jr. (partially hidden), Firestone, Colonel Edmund Starling of the Secret Service and Ford.*

LEFT: *Water splashes in all directions as the riders enter Licking Creek a mile from its entry into the Potomac River in Maryland, July 23. Left to right: Firestone, the President, Colonel Starling and Ford.*

ABOVE: *Edison scans his daily newspaper at Camp Harding, while an informal exchange of thoughts takes place among Ford, the President and Firestone, July 24.*

While Firestone and the President scan the daily newspaper, Edison retires to his favorite form of camp relaxation, July 24.

For several weeks the President's physician, Brigadier General Sawyer, had been urging the President to take more exercise, and among the recreations the doctor advised was horseback riding. So Firestone invited him to take a ride with Ford and himself. The President, borrowing a pair of puttees from one of the grooms, immediately accepted. Harbel, Firestone's favorite riding mount, was brought out and the President, with Ford, Firestone, Harvey junior, George Christian, Jr. and one of the Secret Service agents, Colonel Edmund Starling, went for a canter in the surrounding hills.

Although the President protested that he had not been on a horse for thirty years, his lack of recent experience in no way affected his ability to handle his horse. He rode best when his horse cantered. His seat was good at all times and his pose was easy and natural.

As they swung up one of the roads, a young woman from one of the nearby farmhouses, by the name of Dorothy Murray, came out, waving the American flag. She stopped the party, handing the President a bunch of wildflowers which she had picked especially in his honor, and told him he was the first President of the United States she had ever met. She told Firestone and Ford how important an event the camp had been in her life, as she had never been more than a few miles from her present home and had never expected to meet so many prominent and famous people.

Firestone tries his hand at angling in Licking Creek without success, July 23; Ford surveys the surrounding camping area in Mason's Woods.

Immediately after the ride the President went into a nearby village store to call the White House and inquire about Mrs. Harding's health. The only telephone available was on a party line, and the President had to swing the crank vigorously before he could get the operator and put the call through to Washington. All members of the camping party expressed their pleasure when the President reported that Mrs. Harding's health was improved. As the

President was leaving the store, he found a dozen or so barefoot girls and boys from nearby farms gathered in front and he began to talk with them at once. He invited them all into the store, where he bought candy for each one. So excited were several of the youngsters over the gift that as soon as the President had left, they started running for home with the candy in their hands, apparently intent on saving it as proof of the story they were about to tell their parents—that they had been treated by the President of the United States. [While visiting this campsite in May 1991, the author located Mrs. Carrie Miller, age eighty. As a young girl of ten, while assisting her mother in the local general store, she had waited on the President as he purchased candy for the local youngsters. She noted that Miss Dorothy Murray, age ninety-three, was still living in her farmhouse.—Editor.]

A fishing expedition was next proposed and the fishing rods brought out. After half an hour of fruitless attempts to catch fish from Licking Creek, Edison expressed the feelings of the group when he said, "I don't believe there ever were any fish in this creek." Dinnertime was fast approaching, so Ford grabbed an axe and split firewood, then helped the attendants unpack knives and forks. Fisher and Herman, the chefs, prepared chickens over the hot coals of a good cooking fire. "Hey, folks, come and eat," called Ford. "That isn't the way to say it," corrected Mina Edison. "You should say, 'Come and get it!'" The camping party sat down in the dining tent to a dinner of chicken and Irish stew, corn on the cob, other vegetables, a simple dessert and coffee.

After dinner Ford prepared charcoal smudges to drive away the mosquitos. An electric light plant was trundled out, and a player piano, brought to the camp by a music dealer from Hagerstown, was

ABOVE: *Ford reels in a line while, left to right, Edsel Ford, George Christian, Jr., and Edison study his technique. A cameraman is in view ready to shoot the scene, July 25.*

THE PRESIDENT HARDING CAMP *In the Maryland Mountains* 169

ABOVE: *Enjoying a lunch break are the Edisons and Harvey Firestone, Jr., as they pause near Cumberland, Maryland, while en route to the Swallow Falls campsite, July 27.*

BELOW: *Firestone's saddle horses are loaded into the horse van for their return to Akron, Ohio, as the Edisons wait in the shade of the barn at Camp Harding, July 27.*

started up with a popular dance tune. Several of the campers then gathered on a small platform in the grove. After considerable urging, Ford took a dance lesson from Eleanor Parke Firestone in the then-popular measure called the toddle. "He is wonderful, he learned the first time," she exclaimed to President Harding. "That was because I had such an efficient instructor" was Ford's gallant response.

Loskowski remembered President Harding's coming by and throwing a handful of "take-or-put" spinner tops on a blanket which lay on the ground. He said, "Here, take them all." Loskowski continued, "We each got one, each of the boys got one. I believe I still got mine here yet. I'll never forget that; that was one souvenir I got from the President."

The rest of the evening was spent chatting and listening to Edison spin a few yarns. Ford addressed President Harding as "Mr. President"; he called Edison and Firestone "Tom" and "Harvey"; and they called him "Hank." This first night out with the President was recalled by Loskowski:

"They sat around the fire, we had a big fire, and I had the camp chairs set all around. I'd say the circle was twenty feet or so across. President Harding and Henry Ford sat around the campfire, I guess they didn't go to bed that night until around two o'clock. They sat there and chatted. To tell you the truth, I think Mr. Ford, Mr. Edison and President Harding were the last ones who went to bed that night. I saw that the fire was taken care of, then we went to bed."

The men of the camp arose about six-thirty the next morning, which was Sunday, July 24, and each put a mirror on the nearest tree to shave by, washing up in a tin basin filled from a nearby

ABOVE: *A view of the rolling countryside and rural roadway that led the campers to a western Maryland campsite, near Oakland, July 27.*

spring. The cameramen were on hand to record these morning preparations. After a hearty breakfast, President Harding talked deep-sea fishing in a loud voice to Edison, which gave the mountaineers in the vicinity a chance to hear an authority on the nature and customs of the tarpon.

A flurry of excitement arose, meanwhile, when a truck caught fire from a gasoline range, but the fire was quickly extinguished.

It was time now for the morning canter, and President Harding, Ford, Firestone, George Christian, Jr., Harvey Firestone, Jr. and Colonel Edmund Starling mounted the horses. The President, coatless, led the party and Firestone joined in behind him. They forded Licking Creek, the cameramen recording their passage through the waters. The ride was over, however, in fifteen minutes, after a short canter into the nearby hills.

After a brief rest, at 11 a.m. they attended outdoor Sunday morning services, held by Bishop Anderson. Mrs. Firestone played the piano for the singing of hymns. Several hundred of the nearby farmers and mountaineers attended, as well as a large number of visitors who had come scores of miles that morning to meet the distinguished campers. Bishop Anderson reminded the worshippers that the trees were God's first temple, and the services seemed unusually impressive to those present because of the simple and beautiful natural setting. The bishop chose as his text "Thy Kingdom Come," and explained that although the nineteenth century had been one of nationalism, the twentieth century would be one of internationalism. He referred to the disarmament conference, which President Harding had called as a practical step toward

BELOW: *Luncheon by the roadside just outside Cumberland, Maryland, provides a break in the trip to the second camp on July 27.*

ABOVE: *The camping caravan on the way to western Maryland and a Garrett County campsite at Swallow Falls, July 27.*

BELOW: *Camping vehicles arriving for the second camp at Oakland, Maryland, called Camp Swallow Falls, July 27.*

obtaining peace among the nations. The audience joined President Harding in singing "Rock of Ages" and "Nearer My God to Thee." After the services the President shook hands with the several hundred visitors. When the party again assembled in camp, they found the camp bulldog, Stone, battle-scarred and limping because of a bite on his leg suffered in a battle with a cat. When everyone petted and pampered him, however, he forgot his wounds, wagged his tail and walked about freely. "What he needs," remarked the President, "is mental science."

Shortly thereafter, dinner was announced and the group sat down for its last meal with the President. He expressed his regrets about having to leave, saying that he had hoped to stay longer, but the pressures of affairs of state would not permit it, as the railroad situation was becoming acute. After dinner he chatted with various campers. At 4 p.m. his entourage was organized and he left, shaking hands and assuring everyone that the outing had been a wonderful experience for him. After the President's departure the camp settled down quietly, each member of the party doing as he chose. Early retirement was the choice of all campers after the evening meal.

The campers arose early again on the morning of July 25, and Edison, Ford and Firestone held a conference as to what and where the next move would be. The spot had been so pleasant both in its surroundings and its memories of the President's visit that they decided to stay on there for at least another day; when they announced the decision to the women, there were expressions of pleasure.

That afternoon Mr. and Mrs. Edsel Ford took their departure, driving back to Detroit. The quietness of camplife returned, Ford making his usual sortie into the surrounding countryside in search of any mechanical contrivance or natural resources that he might

come upon. Firestone took his daily horseback ride, accompanied by his sons. Edison, as usual, took a couple of naps during the day and sat for an hour or so after each meal, discussing topics of general interest with his camping companions.

On July 26, Firestone decided to ship the riding horses back to their stables at his home in Akron, Ohio. The next morning, July 27, the horses left by motor truck. Ford, Firestone and Russell were all up to help the grooms load them, the truck departing about seven in the morning. Camp was broken before noon, and the cavalcade of motor cars, led by Edison, got under way for another site in the western Maryland mountains, some ninety miles distant. The route went up through Kaisers Ridge, Maryland, reminiscent of the trip in 1918 when they followed this same highway. And here the residents of Garrett County, who, to a man and woman, knew the great men were not far away and would probably revisit the old campsite, flocked to the sidewalks of Oakland, Maryland. Mrs. James Treacy, an eyewitness to the long procession of cars that filed slowly through the streets of the town, said onlookers wondered whether a circus was coming to town.

From Oakland they branched south off the National Pike and went down toward Deer Park, Maryland, where the party stopped at a roadside field for a late lunch. Just below Deer Park the party turned west on an unimproved road. For nine miles the campers followed this roadway until they reached a lane into a heavily wooded section; they followed the lane for more than a half mile until they came to a beautiful high falls surrounded by a thick grove of pine and fir trees. This is probably the most scenic region in Maryland. Here Muddy Creek flows from the famous Cranesville Pine Swamp and tumbles over a cliff to the bed of a rocky gorge, a drop of some sixty feet. From here it joins Swallow Falls to form the beautiful

ABOVE: *Firestone sits on the thirsty cow pony that was borrowed from a few young people who visited the Swallow Falls camp on Muddy Creek, July 28.*

BELOW: *A cheery campfire provides the setting for memories that last long after the embers die out and the trip is over. This night scene is at Swallow Falls, Maryland.*

ABOVE: *Henry Sines, left, of Sines, Maryland, visits with Russell Firestone and Ford at the Swallow Falls camp.*

Youghiogheny River. Here also is the only extensive stand of virgin timber in Maryland.

Entering this region of whispering pines and hemlocks is like entering a cathedral. There is a solemn stillness in the air, and the dim light which filters through the interlaced branches of the towering trees, some one hundred twenty feet high, is like twilight even on the brightest sunlit day. Twilight deepens into night long before the sun sets. There was a large clearing well suited for pitching tents, but to the disappointment of the party, this site was already occupied by a group of boys from nearby Oakland. Joseph Hinebaugh, one of the boy campers, told how a ten-dollar bill persuaded them to move away to a place nearer Swallow Falls. He said the unexpected manna enabled him and his chums to stay another week. The boys visited the distinguished campers and were treated to candy and other goodies. They had the opportunity to inspect the ingenious way Edison had illuminated the camp. As an alternative to using separate storage batteries, he obtained electric current

for the light bulbs strung around the tents from the automobile batteries.

The first group of cars carrying the campers was able to get over the small light bridge leading to the campsite, but the camp kitchen truck broke through the bridge and blocked the car carrying the food supplies. The entire party helped the crew erect the tents and install the cots, and they just finished as darkness came on. The campfire was built and everyone sat about eating whatever cold food they could from the few tins carried into the camp on foot.

That night the party slept long and arose the next morning an hour later than usual. They found themselves in one of the most secluded spots they had encountered on their trips. No cars could get to them because of the broken bridge, and no visitors except the youngsters who had set up camp nearby came to see them that day. The camp suited Edison "to the ground." He sat for hours in his camp chair viewing the falls and the river, discussing all kinds of topics. Firestone was an attentive listener as Ford told amusing sto-

ABOVE: *Passenger cars negotiate the muddy road while leaving the Oakland, Maryland, camp at Swallow Falls, July 31.*

LEFT: *Heavy July rains turned the roads into a quagmire and the heavy equipment had to be towed out.*

ABOVE: *The crew is setting up the third camp at Cheat River near Elkins, West Virginia, August 1.*

ries about his youthful struggles, and they both encouraged Edison to tell tales of his early days as a "butcher," selling candy and magazines on a commuter train to Detroit. He also told how, in the course of chemical experiments, he set fire to the baggage car and received a dishonorable discharge for it.

The campers bathed and swam in the pools of Swallow Falls on July 28 and hiked along the trails between the separated falls. Had John Burroughs lived to join his fellow campers once again, he most certainly would have been excited to be so close to the Cranesville Pine Swamp, a strange boreal pocket of plants and animals that had been driven southward by the great glacier of the Ice Age, but which stayed in this five-hundred-acre tract after most of the arctic life had retreated northward with the receding glacier. This geological freak is in an almost inaccessible area. In spite of his physical absence, John Burroughs's indomitable spirit pervaded the camp.

Ford, while scouting for anything old and mechanical on the backwoods roads, spied an old steam engine at a sawmill. Ford left word that he wanted to buy the engine. The following day the engine's owner, Newton Reams, went to the camp to see Ford.

"Are you kidding me or do you really want to buy my steam engine?" he asked.

"I am certainly not kidding you," replied Ford. "How much do you want for it?" When Reams said one hundred dollars, Ford's hand went into his pocket and out came two new fifty-dollar bills. After inspecting the engine and explaining how it could be altered to deliver more power, Ford noticed that a small part was missing and asked Reams whether he could get a replacement. He told Ford he thought he could find the part at another mill nearby. When Reams approached the neighbor to buy the part, he was told that part was not for sale, but the engine was.

ABOVE: *Lunchtime at Camp Cheat, West Virginia. Seated at the dining table, are left to right, Mrs. William Anderson, Mrs. Harvey Firestone, Sr., Harvey Firestone, Sr., Mrs. Harvey Firestone, Jr., Harvey Firestone, Jr., Mrs. Thomas Edison and Thomas Edison, August 1.*

"How much?" asked Reams. "Seventy-five dollars."

So Reams hurried back to tell Ford about the other engine, which was complete in every detail.

"How much?" asked Ford.

Reams upped the price to $150. Again the hand of the auto tycoon went into his pocket, this time extracting three fifty-dollar bills. Reams took both engines to Oakland, where they were loaded onto a boxcar and shipped to Dearborn, Michigan.

Another sortie into the surrounding territory, with an engineer whom Ford had brought along, revealed several old-fashioned boilers and sawmill equipment abandoned years before when the log industry had left that part of the country. Ford himself made sketches of this machinery and took some of it apart to examine more closely.

On this visit Ford's Lincoln became mired in the mud, according to a local story. As horses were being hitched to the car to pull it out of the muck, a small boy, who did not know Ford, said, "Mister, you have the wrong kind of car. My father drives a Ford and it never gets stuck on this road." Ford was pleased by the remark, so he took out a pencil and notebook and wrote down the name and address of the boy's father. A brand-new Ford car later was delivered to the family.

One of the most interesting visitors to the camp was a seventy-five-year-old mountaineer, Henry Sines, who lived two miles away on a farm that had been his home all his life. He described conditions in that part of the country fifty years before and made an impression on the entire camping party with his tales of the hardships which had to be overcome in pioneer farming in the mountains.

Certainly R. Emerson Cross and his chums, who were out for a day's frolic on horses they had rented in Oakland, were astonished when they rode into a clearing near Muddy Creek Falls and

ABOVE: *Ford hangs up his wash to dry in the midsummer sunlight at the Cheat River camp.*

found it buzzing with activity. They quickly learned who the campers were, and were politely invited to visit the camp. While Cross, later a special police officer at the White House, and his friends inspected the elaborate camp setup, Firestone, Harvey junior and his wife, Russell Firestone and other vivacious members of the camping party requested the loan of the horses. Permission was granted, and when the riders returned, the boys from Oakland were handed crisp bank bills, some tens and some twenties. Since the boys had paid only a dollar and a quarter each for the use of the horses for the entire day, they were elated. The enthusiastic account the boys gave when they returned to Oakland spread the news of the arrival of the celebrated company, and many of the local residents flocked out to behold the wonders in their neighborhood.

On July 29, the campers were ready to confer about when to move on to another campsite, but the matter became moot the following day, July 30, when a very heavy rainstorm came up lasting for hours. The narrow trail out to the highway became so muddy that the cars could not be moved. Later in the afternoon the weather began to clear; however, it was not possible yet to move the camp, because the roads were still impassable.

Edison thought the campers should see the Cheat River district. Therefore, the bridge having been repaired, on July 31 the party struck camp, and started out to seek another site. Fred Loskowski related his experience in trying to negotiate the roads with the big White truck which carried the camping equipment:

"We pulled onto some of those mud roads there. It had rained, and the red clay–Lord God! I had an awful time getting up with that big White truck. In fact, a guy who had bought a new Fordson tractor helped me. I had to walk three-quarters of a mile. I had slid over into the ditch. Of course, the others had gone on. They had smaller cars, so they could make it up the hill. I went up and asked the man and he said, 'I'll drive the truck if you drive the tractor. I won't pull you up that hill. We'll tip it over this way.' I said, 'No, it won't.' So he drove the truck, and I drove the tractor up the hill. I pulled myself up. It was just greasy. The truck could go all right, but it was just so greasy the tires couldn't make it. I pulled it up to the top of the hill. I gave the man five dollars for his trouble, and I went to catch up with the folks."

It was late in the afternoon when they arrived at Elkins, West Virginia. The camp equipment did not come along until later and it was not possible to locate a good campsite, so they rented quarters in the hotel for Sunday night.

Next morning, August 1, Mr. and Mrs. Harvey Firestone, Jr., and Russell Firestone left the party to go to Washington, D.C. Members of the crew came to advise that they had located a camping place a few miles away. Ford, Edison and Firestone journeyed

ABOVE: *An aerial view of the Cheat River Valley.*

out to the site, which became the camp at Cheat River. This proved to be just an overnight camp. As Ford's and Firestone's offices had been inquiring more frequently of late concerning their return, it was decided that they would start back home.

On August 2, rain at Wheeling, West Virginia caused the camping party to change their plans and they headed northward, passing through Fairmont, West Virginia, before stopping for a roadside lunch and then proceeding through Morgantown to finally arrive at the Summit Hotel near Uniontown, Pennsylvania. The evening, being the last they could spend together on this trip, brought out much conversation.

Edison capped the evening as he demonstrated his agility by kicking a cigar off the mantle in the hotel lobby three straight times, while Ford was able to connect just once. A stair-jumping contest followed as Ford bounced up ten steps in two hops, Edison needed three hops.

After a rather late breakfast, the party moved out to Uniontown, arriving there about noon on August 3. They stopped on Morgantown Street for a few minutes before continuing on the final leg of the 1921 camping trip, to Pittsburgh, Pennsylvania. Mr. and Mrs. Edison left Pittsburgh by auto for their return to West Orange, New Jersey. Mr. and Mrs. Harvey Firestone, Sr., and Mr. and Mrs. Henry Ford, with their respective entourages, continued northward to their homes. Thus ended one of the most exciting, interesting and memorable trips the campers had experienced together so far.

ER PENINSULA

1923

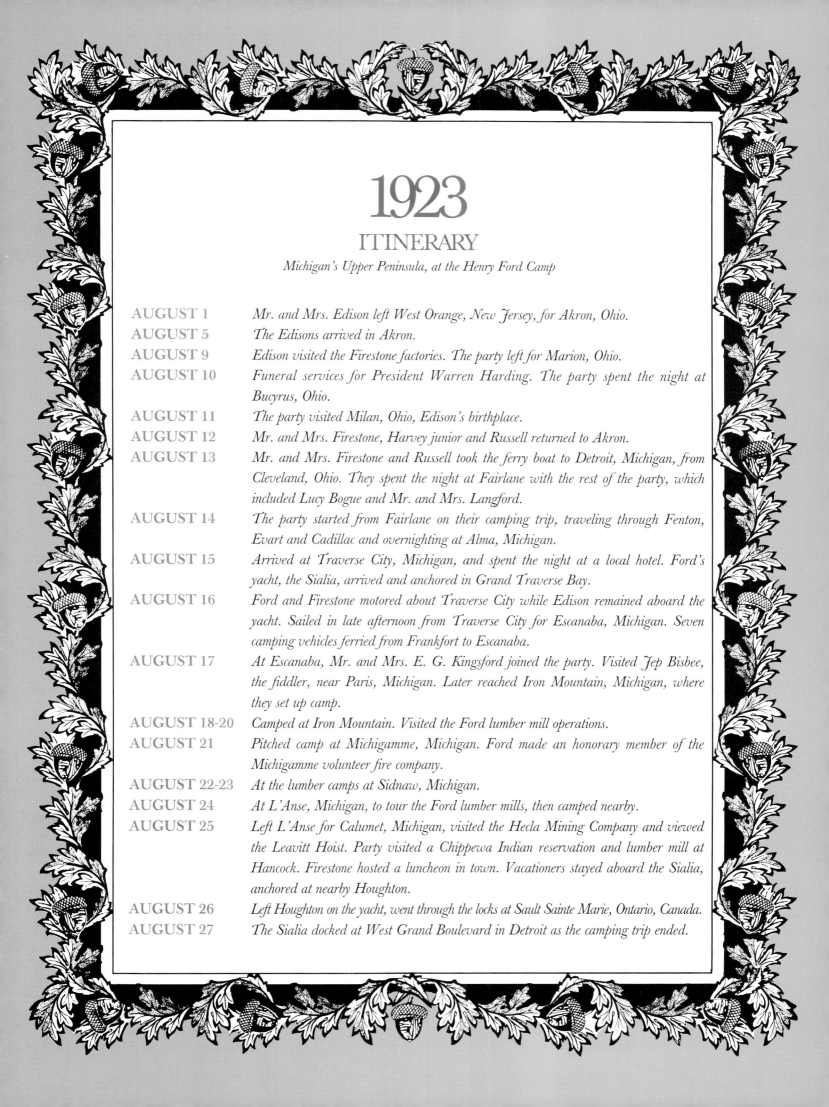

1923
ITINERARY

Michigan's Upper Peninsula, at the Henry Ford Camp

AUGUST 1	*Mr. and Mrs. Edison left West Orange, New Jersey, for Akron, Ohio.*
AUGUST 5	*The Edisons arrived in Akron.*
AUGUST 9	*Edison visited the Firestone factories. The party left for Marion, Ohio.*
AUGUST 10	*Funeral services for President Warren Harding. The party spent the night at Bucyrus, Ohio.*
AUGUST 11	*The party visited Milan, Ohio, Edison's birthplace.*
AUGUST 12	*Mr. and Mrs. Firestone, Harvey junior and Russell returned to Akron.*
AUGUST 13	*Mr. and Mrs. Firestone and Russell took the ferry boat to Detroit, Michigan, from Cleveland, Ohio. They spent the night at Fairlane with the rest of the party, which included Lucy Bogue and Mr. and Mrs. Langford.*
AUGUST 14	*The party started from Fairlane on their camping trip, traveling through Fenton, Evart and Cadillac and overnighting at Alma, Michigan.*
AUGUST 15	*Arrived at Traverse City, Michigan, and spent the night at a local hotel. Ford's yacht, the Sialia, arrived and anchored in Grand Traverse Bay.*
AUGUST 16	*Ford and Firestone motored about Traverse City while Edison remained aboard the yacht. Sailed in late afternoon from Traverse City for Escanaba, Michigan. Seven camping vehicles ferried from Frankfort to Escanaba.*
AUGUST 17	*At Escanaba, Mr. and Mrs. E. G. Kingsford joined the party. Visited Jep Bisbee, the fiddler, near Paris, Michigan. Later reached Iron Mountain, Michigan, where they set up camp.*
AUGUST 18-20	*Camped at Iron Mountain. Visited the Ford lumber mill operations.*
AUGUST 21	*Pitched camp at Michigamme, Michigan. Ford made an honorary member of the Michigamme volunteer fire company.*
AUGUST 22-23	*At the lumber camps at Sidnaw, Michigan.*
AUGUST 24	*At L'Anse, Michigan, to tour the Ford lumber mills, then camped nearby.*
AUGUST 25	*Left L'Anse for Calumet, Michigan, visited the Hecla Mining Company and viewed the Leavitt Hoist. Party visited a Chippewa Indian reservation and lumber mill at Hancock. Firestone hosted a luncheon in town. Vacationers stayed aboard the Sialia, anchored at nearby Houghton.*
AUGUST 26	*Left Houghton on the yacht, went through the locks at Sault Sainte Marie, Ontario, Canada.*
AUGUST 27	*The Sialia docked at West Grand Boulevard in Detroit as the camping trip ended.*

ABOVE: *An aft view of the Sialia in Grand Traverse Bay, the national ensign flying proudly, August 15.*

1923

MICHIGAN'S UPPER PENINSULA

"At the Henry Ford Camp"

I n 1922 the famous trio made no camping trip together. In the summer of 1923, however, they decided to revive their annual outing. Newspapers announced on August 1, 1923, that Mr. and Mrs. Thomas Edison had left West Orange, New Jersey, for Akron, Ohio, where they would join the Harvey Firestones. The Edisons and Firestones would then meet the Henry Fords in Detroit, Michigan. People at once jumped to the conclusion—correctly—that another camping trip was in the making.

The Edisons arrived in Akron on August 5, and spent the next three days visiting with the Firestone family. On August 9 Edison visited the Firestone factories in Akron, where he received a hearty reception from the people of the Firestone organization.

Meanwhile, word had come that President Warren G. Harding had passed away while on a vacation trip to the West Coast, and that funeral services would be held at his home in Marion, Ohio, on August 10. This sad news was unexpected, and most likely brought to mind the happy days just two years earlier when the President had joined the group in Maryland.

The Edisons, Mr. and Mrs. Firestone, Harvey junior and Russell Firestone motored at once to Marion, where they were the guests the night of August 9 of Mrs. George W. King, widow of the head of the Marion Steam Shovel Works. They were joined by Henry Ford, who came from Detroit to attend the funeral. Bishop William F. and Mrs. Anderson, who were members of the camping party in 1921, also arrived in Marion for the funeral services.

The Edisons, Firestones, Ford and Mrs. King drove up to the Harding residence at 10:45 a.m. on August 10 to pay their final respects to their friend, then went to the cemetery and sat inside the roped area before the vault until the funeral cortege arrived.

After the service the party went to the Marion Club, where they had lunch. Upon emerging from the club at 1 p.m., they were surrounded by hundreds of people who had assembled to get a glimpse of them. Army officers, commanding troops who were in the city for the funeral, suspected a disturbance and came

ABOVE: *Henry Ford's residence, Fairlane, in Dearborn, Michigan, where three camping support vehicles stand in formation ready for the 1923 trip to the Upper Peninsula of Michigan and a visit to Ford's lumber mills, August 14.*

running, only to join the throng of admirers.

When the party reached Etowah, the King residence, newspaper reporters and cameramen swooped down upon them. The newsmen persuaded Edison to voice his thoughts on the soul, because the funeral of the President naturally caused the mind to dwell on this metaphysical phenomenon. "There is a great directing head of things and people—a Supreme Being who looks after the destinies of the world," Edison declared. "I have faith in a Supreme Being, and all my thoughts are regarding life after death—where the soul goes, what form it takes and its relation to those now living. I am convinced that the body is made up of entities which are intelligent. When one cuts his finger, I believe it is intelligence of these entities that heals the wound. When one is sick, it is intelligence of these entities that brings convalescence.

"You know that there are living cells in the body so tiny that the microscope cannot show them at all. The entity that gives life and motion to the human body is finer still and lies infinitely beyond the reach of our finest scientific instruments. When the entity deserts the body, the body is like a ship without a rudder—deserted, motionless and dead. It is mere clay, as all orthodox Christians believe. I still believe in the religion of our Lord and Master," Edison declared.

The Edisons, the Firestones and Ford left Marion late in the day for Bucyrus, en route to Milan, Ohio, Edison's birthplace. They took lodging for the night at Elberson's Hotel in Bucyrus. After a hearty breakfast of ham and eggs at the hotel, the following morning the visitors got into their autos and started for Milan at 9 a.m. on August 11.

The party as it left Bucyrus was composed of the Edisons, Ford, The Firestones (including Harvey Jr. and Russell), W. D. Hines and Margaret Miller. The first thing Edison did on his arrival in Milan was to visit the brick house in which he was born, which was on the

outskirts of town. He found the house spic and span from cellar to garret. Etta Wadsworth, daughter of the late Mrs. Nancy Wadsworth, whom Edison termed "a favorite cousin," awaited him at the door with a number of friends and neighbors.

Edison and his friends then went to the Milan Library where Judge R. H. Williams, a native of Milan, extended a formal welcome to Edison on behalf of the town. Almost the entire population of Milan, which at the time was about twelve hundred, and hundreds of other people from within a radius of twenty-five miles had assembled in the public square to see the famous inventor and his traveling companions.

Edison responded briefly to the welcome from Judge Williams and said that he was glad to get back to Milan once more and that he would have been back before had he not been so busy. Henry Ford, when introduced, said briefly, "I have heard so much, I don't know what to say." Harvey Firestone acted as a spokesman for the party during the reception by saying, "You people of Milan may well be proud of your distinguished son. Mr. Edison is unquestionably the greatest man of his generation. I am glad to be with my two great friends on this camping trip. I know we are going to have a good time."

The village brass band then rendered a program, including among their numbers "Hail! Hail! The Gang's All Here!" The villagers and visitors in the meantime passed before the guests and shook their hands.

On the afternoon of August 12 the party motored to the old Hiram Page farm, between Milan and Huron, Ohio, to be dinner guests of Mrs. Edward Wheeler. Mrs. Page, wife of the original owner of this farm, was Edison's sister, with whom Edison had spent several weeks each summer after his parents moved from Milan to Port Huron, Michigan.

ABOVE: *Ford's yacht, the Sialia, sits at anchor in Grand Traverse Bay, Lake Michigan, ready to transfer the camping party to Escanaba, Michigan, August 16.*

BELOW: *Walter McLean, the captain of the Sialia. The yacht, which was 300 feet long, had a crew of thirty hands, three of whom were in constant contact with the outside world by wireless, August 15.*

The visit to the Page farm marked the end of the sojourn around Milan, and the party made plans for a trip to northern Michigan which would complete their annual outing. It was agreed that they would reassemble at Fairlane, Ford's home near Dearborn, the following day for the trip, which Ford was to host.

Mr. and Mrs. Firestone and their son Russell left Akron on August 13 and took the ferryboat across Lake Erie from Cleveland to Detroit. They joined the rest of the assemblage at Fairlane. Lucy Bogue (Mrs. Edison's friend), and Mr. Langford (Henry Ford's cousin), and his wife had, in the meantime, become members of the group, which was headed for the camping trail on the Upper Peninsula of northern Michigan.

On the following day, August 14, the real camping trip began and the party set forth from Fairlane well fortified with food, helpers and attendants. Three Lincoln cars carried members of the party, and there were, in addition, a truck, two camp trucks filled with tents and cots and a photographer in a Ford auto.

Russell Firestone drove his mother and father in one Lincoln with a destination of Pontiac, Michigan. They unfortunately got on the wrong road to Pontiac and were separated from the party. They knew, however, that a rendezvous was planned for Traverse City, Michigan, so they inquired at Pontiac as to the best road there. En

route they drove through Fenton, Evart, Cadillac and Alma, stopping overnight at Alma.

They drove all the next day, August 15, until reaching Traverse City, where they made plans to stay overnight and await the arrival of the rest of the entourage. After registering at a local hotel, Firestone and Russell took an evening stroll uptown. On their way back to the hotel they noticed some trucks coming down the street; as the trucks passed, they recognized them as belonging to their party. Russell immediately ran after the trucks, caught up with them and jumped on Ford's car. The group then drove to the hotel, where they joined Mrs. Firestone. Ford's yacht, the *Sialia*, had arrived and lay at anchor in Grand Traverse Bay.

On the following day, August 16, the *Sialia* ferried the party to Ford's Island, an uninhabited island in Grand Traverse Bay, three miles from the mainland. Upon his arrival in Traverse City, Ford had identified the island as an ideal camping site. The original intention had been to camp on the island during the day and sleep on the *Sialia* at night, then be ferried to and from the island in the morning and evening aboard the accompanying cabin cruiser. These plans were changed, however, and it was decided to take the yacht later in the day directly from Traverse City to Escanaba, Michigan. In the meantime Ford and Firestone motored about Traverse City while

ABOVE: *A view of the camp at Iron Mountain, an ideal location on the Upper Peninsula of Michigan, August 18.*

BELOW: *A pensive Henry Ford relaxes for a moment in his sombrero and bandanna.*

ABOVE: *Edison smiles, probably in disbelief, at the getup on Ford and E.G. Kingsford as they strike a desperado pose at the L'Anse camp, August 24.*

ABOVE: *Firestone demonstrates the art of adapting to primitive conditions as he prepares to shave in the wilderness of the Iron Mountain camp, August 19.*

Edison stayed aboard the yacht.

The *Sialia* sailed out of Traverse Bay for Escanaba, Michigan, late in the afternoon with the camping group on board. The yacht was a graceful sight as it glided along. It was three hundred feet long, had every known safety device and was adapted and equipped for comfort. The ship had a crew of thirty, three of whom, in shifts, provided constant wireless service. The seven vehicles were driven to Frankfort, Michigan, to be loaded on a car ferry that would convey them to Escanaba.

Langford was especially fond of dancing, and so the party passed the evening's voyage on Lake Michigan in dancing. Following a foggy night, the yacht dropped anchor at Escanaba early on the

morning of August 17, and the group went ashore. The cars were waiting, and the caravan left Escanaba for Iron Mountain, Michigan, at 10 a.m.

E. G. Kingsford, who was manager of the Ford operations on the Upper Peninsula, and his wife joined the party at this juncture. Kingsford suggested that they visit Jep Bisbee, a famous old-time fiddler who lived in Paris, Michigan, near Iron Mountain. Paris was a crossroads village not used to the sight of a caravan of cars driven by men in khaki uniforms. A crowd gathered to give the campers the once-over, and somebody suggested that the man in the back seat looked like Henry Ford. "By George, it is him," said another. "And that must be Mrs. Ford, and say, I read that Thomas Edison and Harvey Firestone are with him. That's them! By George, it is!"

The crowd was asked whether anyone knew the way to Jep Bisbee's house. The assemblage pointed the way. In a moment Mrs. Bisbee, seventy-seven years old, was smiling on the doorstep of her home and saying, "I will go and get my husband and have him play for you, come right in." And then Jep Bisbee played. He fiddled the old reels, the old quickstep and the old jig. He played and called square dances that were popular fifty years earlier. The visitors heard the kind of music that was nearly impossible to hear at that time. Edison moved closer to Jep Bisbee to see whether his measures and accent were right, and he seemed satisfied that the old fiddler made no mistakes.

ABOVE: *Left to right: Mrs. Edward Kingsford, Clara Ford and Mina Edison share a moment after lunch at the Iron Mountain camp, August 20.*

BELOW: *Ford manager E. G. Kingsford discusses the pros and cons of the native wood supply at the Iron Mountain mill site for Ford and Edison, on his right and Firestone, on his left.*

ABOVE: *The villagers provided a warm welcome as the travelers stopped at a general store in Paris, Michigan. Jep Bisbee, the fiddler, was paid a visit here on August 17.*

ABOVE: *Firestone checks out his newly developed balloon tires after a grueling test on the roadways of the Upper Peninsula. The results appear quite satisfactory.*

For a time the revelers were carried back to a period when this kind of music was popular. "It seems so good to hear that," said someone in the audience. The visitors were so impressed that Ford, an avid collector, purchased one of Bisbee's old violins and Edison expressed the wish that the fiddler visit West Orange, New Jersey, so that his tunes might be recorded on phonograph records. Ford, upon his return home, had a car shipped to Bisbee in appreciation, and the fiddler eventually did come to record for Edison.

The party chose a grove near the Ford lumber mill at Iron Mountain as the site for their camp. Ford owned five hundred thousand acres of timber in this vicinity and this lumber mill was one of his best. Consequently, the party spent considerable time going through the Ford mill. The Iron Mountain sawmill made all the

woodwork for the closed bodies of the Ford autos right at the forest, saving the costs of transporting waste lumber. Conservation plans included cutting only trees over ten inches in diameter, and all brush was cleared out to promote new growth and to prevent forest fires. A plant converted waste wood into valuable chemicals and charcoal. Of course, Edison was in his element, and he and Ford developed process after process, most of which were placed into operation here.

Ford's three cardinal rules of manufacture became very clear upon close examination of this operation. The first rule was to avoid transportation of useless materials. The second was to quicken the turnover of assets. And the third was to earn from waste materials. Not lost on Firestone was Ford's concept that a manufacturing operation should be carried through without a stop from raw materials to finished product, and that to be in control of his business a manufacturer must control his sources.

During the day Ford strolled about the town, made friends with the local children and talked with his workers in the mill. Firestone spent much of his spare time testing the balloon tires on his car to see how they stood up under adverse road and weather conditions. It was at this time that balloon tires were first being developed.

The campers spent three days going through the mill at Iron Mountain, where the various processes were perfected in the inimitable Ford manner. The manager of the mill and his wife, along with

ABOVE: The spit and polish appearance of the interior of a cabin at the Sidnaw lumber camp, August 22.

BELOW: A row of cabins for the lumberjacks at Ford's lumber camp at Sidnaw, Michigan, August 22.

ABOVE: *Russell Firestone watches intently as Ford sights a target for a practice shot at a bull's-eye at the Sidnaw lumber camp, August 22.*

ABOVE: *A semiformal pose is struck by members of the camping party at Sidnaw. Front, Mrs. Edward Kingsford, Harvey and Russell Firestone; rear, Clara and Henry Ford, Thomas and Mina Edison, Edward Kingsford and Idabelle Firestone, August 23.*

BELOW: *Firestone discusses a matter with Edison at the Ford lumber mill at L'Anse, Michigan.*

Mrs. Langford, were dinner guests at the camp, while the party continued to enjoy the rugged environment of Iron Mountain.

Camp was struck on August 21 and the campers motored to Michigamme, Michigan, where a delightful spot was selected for the tents near Lake Michigamme. Although a steady drizzle kept the campers in their tents most of the day, the weather cleared sufficiently for the Fords to walk through the streets of the village. Mrs. Ford noticed a group of girls from nearby Camp Cha-Ton-Ka, who had turned out to greet the visitors wearing cutoff overalls with their stockings rolled down to reveal their knees. Mrs. Ford expressed strong disapproval, refusing to give autographs to persons in such attire. Newspaper people immediately latched onto the "dimpled-knee" controversy, but Mrs. Ford firmly stood her ground. Somewhat later on their stroll Ford noticed puffs of smoke coming from under the veranda of an abandoned hospital building. He found a large pail and ran with it to the edge of the nearby lake, where he filled the bucket and extinguished the flames. The news of this exploit quickly spread throughout Michigamme and Ford was made an honorary member of the Michigamme volunteer fire company.

Before the party left Michigamme to continue its itinerary, Ford took a few minutes to inspect his Imperial Mine just west of the village. From here the campers motored some thirty miles westward to Sidnaw, Michigan, where Ford owned some more lumber camps.

These proved to be a revelation to the camping party—all were fitted with wicker furniture, hardwood floors, varnished walls, hot and cold running water and shower baths. Rumor had it that Ford encouraged his lumberjacks to take a bath every Saturday night, whether they needed it or not.

The lumber camp at Sidnaw, where the camping party made their headquarters on August 22 and 23, consisted of four shacks for sleeping quarters for the lumberjacks, a shack fitted out as a kitchen for the storage and preparation of food and four guest houses. The party stayed at the guest houses, which were heated by a steam system. The warmth of the cabins was a decided comfort because the weather had turned raw and cold. Drizzling rains kept the group indoors much of the time. Edison read a great deal, and when weather permitted took walks and closely inspected the trees and lumber.

From Sidnaw the party went on to L'Anse, Michigan, August 24,

TOP: *The campers, while observing the operations at the L'Anse lumber mill, were impressed with the log cars on the railroad siding, here seen at left. The car beds tilted, allowing the logs to roll on an inclined plane into the holding pond. The workmen then poled the logs into the adjacent mill.*

ABOVE: *Firestone, dressed for the chill in the air, prepares to board one of the vehicles for a tour of the lumber mill facilities at Sidnaw, August 23.*

LEFT: *The crew members line up in military fashion with their respective camping vehicles at the L'Anse, Michigan, lumber mill on the Upper Peninsula, August 24.*

where Ford had located more sawmills. The weather became so cold that everyone put on heavy mackinaws and boots, which were customarily worn on the Upper Peninsula for added protection and warmth. Russell Firestone drove the men of the party to view Ford's vast property and lumber holdings in the vicinity of the camp. In the meantime, Kingsford's son, while en route to Iron Mountain, came down to L'Anse with his young bride and joined the camping party. The following morning young Kingsford and Russell Firestone went hunting, but failed to bag any game. On their return to camp, the men engaged in a shooting contest.

The entourage left L'Anse on August 25, in crisp late-summer weather on their way to Calumet, Michigan, at the extreme upper tip of the peninsula, where they spent the day inspecting the mining machinery of the Calumet Hecla Mining Company. Here the officers of the organization gave a luncheon at their club in honor of the members of the camping party.

At Calumet, the giant Leavitt hoist was located, and this was minutely examined by the trio. The inventor of the hoist was known to both Edison and Ford. While here in Calumet, the party lived on the Ford yacht, which was nearby at anchor on Lake Superior. The yacht had taken the water route from Escanaba through the locks at Sault Sainte Marie, Ontario, Canada, and dropped anchor at

Houghton, Michigan, which lies close below Calumet. The accompanying cabin cruiser ferried the guests to and from the shore. The party took drives through the vicinity, which proved to be very beautiful country. On one side trip they visited the Chippewa Indian reservation outside Hancock, Michigan. Ford had another lumber mill at Hancock and wanted to see a member of the reservation about some property. Later Firestone hosted a luncheon party at a noted inn in town.

Russell Firestone, who had a prior commitment, left the rest of the party at L'Anse, and motored down to Chicago, Illinois. The other members had traveled by auto to Houghton to board the yacht, and after enjoying activities there headed through the Straights to Keweenaw Bay and on toward their destination of Detroit.

When the news reached Sault Sainte Marie, on August 26 that the *Sialia* had reached the locks, hundreds of tourists and local citizens lined the docks to watch the yacht's progress. As the *Sialia* was locked through, Edison, Ford and Firestone stood on the deck. While the yacht was tied up for a few moments at the pier in preparation to go through Poe Lock, Ford stepped ashore and greeted the tourists. A shout came from the yacht that it was time to move on, and Ford yelled, "Let 'er go!" The crowd then witnessed Ford run like a boy in pursuit of the ship, some five hundred feet away, and leap aboard.

The return trip to Detroit was enjoyable but uneventful. The *Sialia* docked at the foot of West Grand Boulevard in the Detroit River late the next day. Because of the late hour, the party abandoned a proposed visit to the River Rouge plant of the Ford Motor Company and left for Fairlane, Ford's home at Dearborn.

The trip had been a complete success. The camping journey had covered over four thousand miles, while Ford had proven to be a perfect host. Mrs. Edison summed it all up when she said the trip had been full of pleasure because "We studied the country, then chose the best season."

Fred Loskowski, would recall later:

"Mr. Ford would be a changed man after these trips—noticeably refreshed and rested. He was just living another life, just like we'd be—turn us loose in the wilderness and live and have fun and everything out there. That's what I say, he had a wonderful time. A new man—he had refreshed himself. He had met all his friends there and they had a wonderful talk and things like that. After each trip he never talked about them. He never said anything, at least to me, he never said a word to me about nothing until time came when he wanted to go again."

ABOVE: *Firestone lunches with a Chippewa Indian family near Hancock, Michigan, August 24.*

1924

ITINERARY

The Wayside Inn Trip, a Visit to President Calvin Coolidge

AUGUST 10   *Harvey Firestone, Sr., and Russell Firestone left Akron, Ohio, for the Wayside Inn at South Sudbury, Massachusetts.*

AUGUST 12   *The Firestones arrived at the Wayside Inn during the evening.*

AUGUST 13   *Ford hosted the Middlesex County Farm Bureau and Extension Service picnic. Mr. and Mrs. Edison arrived at the Wayside Inn that night.*

AUGUST 14   *Remained at the Wayside Inn until August 16. Benjamin Lovett demonstrated the old-fashioned mazurkas and polkas.*

AUGUST 17   *Russell Firestone met with President Calvin Coolidge's secretary, Bascom Slemp, and arranged for the party to call on the President on Tuesday, August 19.*

AUGUST 18   *Left for Ludlow, Vermont, and stopped at the Okemo Tavern for dinner and lodgings.*

AUGUST 19   *Arrived in Plymouth, Vermont, at 11 a.m., called on President and Mrs. Coolidge and the President's father, Colonel John Coolidge and toured local cheese factory. Left for Woodstock, Vermont and Concord, New Hampshire. Arrived in Portsmouth, New Hampshire, and spent the night on the Sialia in Portsmouth harbor.*

AUGUST 20   *The Edisons left for Bretton Woods, New Hampshire, in the White Mountains. Ford and the Firestones visited Exeter, New Hampshire. The Fords sailed for Seal Harbor, Maine, to visit Edsel Ford and his family. The Firestones drove to Mount Washington.*

AUGUST 21   *The Firestones spent the day golfing at Mount Washington.*

AUGUST 22   *The Firestones left for Albany, New York, to catch the train for Akron, Ohio. The Edisons visited Montpelier and Rutland, Vermont.*

AUGUST 23   *The Firestones arrived in Akron, Ohio.*

AUGUST 27   *The Edisons returned to West Orange, New Jersey.*

ABOVE: *Thomas and Mina Edison, seated, and Firestone, Clara and Henry Ford, standing, pose for an informal portrait at Longfellow's Wayside Inn.*

1924
THE WAYSIDE INN TRIP
"A Visit to President Calvin Coolidge"

Instead of camping out in the open, as had been their custom on vacation trips during previous summers, the traveling entrepreneurs decided in 1924 to locate at the Wayside Inn at South Sudbury, Massachusetts, and to use the inn as a point of departure for side trips in the vicinity. Henry Ford had acquired the inn the previous year and now proposed to be the host for this summer's get-together.

With the outing plans in mind, Harvey Firestone and his son Russell left Akron, Ohio, on August 10, 1924, with South Sudbury as their ultimate destination. They arrived on August 12 and were assigned to the French Poet's Room. The Fords, having preceded the rest of the party, were already at the inn. Thomas Edison and his wife were expected on the following day, to complete the group of vacationers.

Ford was up before nine o'clock the next morning, August 13, and after a short walk about the adjacent farmland with Russell Firestone, had breakfast with his wife and the Firestones in the common dining room of the inn. The food served in the hostelry was grown on the farm near the inn, and so the public who patronized the inn's dining room enjoyed fresh vegetables, chickens and eggs. The homegrown food products of raw vegetables, raw milk, whole wheat cereals and like items were part of a dietary regimen taken up by Ford.

That day was the day of the Middlesex County Farm Bureau and Extension Service picnic, and Ford had thrown open the Wayside Inn and his farm as a site for the outing. By the time the party finished breakfast, farmers had begun to arrive at the inn from all parts of Middlesex County. When Ford went to the old-fashioned flower garden at the side of the inn, the farmers gathered around him. Ford liked to talk to people individually, but not in crowds; he would ask this farmer, then that one, about his farm and crops.

There was much of interest for the three thousand picnickers at the Wayside Inn, and they inspected every nook and cranny of the tavern and explored its grounds. The famous inn was at its

THE STORY OF THE WAYSIDE INN

THE WAYSIDE INN WAS LOCATED ON THE BAY PATH, WHICH LATER BECAME KNOWN AS THE Boston Post Road. This path was used by coastal families for journeys to the inland wilderness. Strategically located between Boston, Massachusetts, and Hartford, Connecticut, along a stage line established in the 1780s by Captain Levi Pease, the Wayside Inn had long been a convenient resting place for weary travelers.

In 1702 David How (then the spelling) constructed the beginnings of the present inn on 130 acres which had been granted to him by his father, Samuel. David's grandfather John, from 1661 to 1702, had operated the Black Horse Tavern in Marlborough, a small town to the west of Sudbury.

Ezekiel Howe, David's son, became proprietor in 1746 and subsequently named the hostelry the Red Horse Tavern. He was a colonel in the local minutemen militia during the Revolutionary War; upon his death in 1796 his son Adam, a fifth-generation Howe, became the innkeeper. By then the inn was the center of social life in Sudbury and surrounding towns. Adam retired in 1830 and relinquished his position as proprietor to his son Lyman.

Henry Wadsworth Longfellow visited the inn on at least two occasions after Lyman's death in 1861. He gained knowledge of the locale by sitting around the cheery fireplace and chatting with literary and learned gentlemen, through talking with others who had stopped at the inn and by interviewing townspeople. Longfellow drew on these stories and tales when, in 1863, he published his *Tales of a Wayside Inn*. Lyman Howe took his place as the landlord in perhaps the best-known story of them all, "Listen, my children, and you shall hear of the midnight ride of Paul Revere."

Edward Lemon purchased the inn in 1897 and, recognizing the value of the Longfellow association, renamed it Longfellow's Wayside Inn.

In 1923 an Association of Friends of the Inn was formed in recognition of the need to preserve the historic building. That was when Henry Ford, who had a deep respect for the principles of our founding fathers, coupled with a taste for old buildings, furniture, antiques and farm equipment, came forward to preserve this fine example of Colonial America. Ford later purchased five thousand acres around the inn to preserve its setting.

In 1926 Ford arranged for the transfer of the Red Stone School from Sterling, Massachusetts, to Sudbury. This schoolhouse, built in 1798, was made famous by the rhyme "Mary Had a Little Lamb," which was written by John Roulstone about classmate Mary E. Sawyer. Beyond the school, Ford erected a traditional nondenominational chapel named Martha-Mary in honor of his mother and Clara Ford's mother. A gristmill was added there in 1929. It is powered by water from little Hop Brook, with the water flowing over an eighteen-foot overshot wheel.

Fire struck the inn on December 22, 1955, gutting the north and west wings. A monumental restoration task was undertaken, and after exhaustive research the inn came back to life much as it previously was, from the original concept through numerous additions and remodelings. Incredibly, nearly eighty percent of the furnishings, artifacts and antiques were spared from the flames as more than one million gallons of water were used to extinguish the fire.

LEFT: *Middlesex County, Massachusetts, farmers and their wives, some strolling, some just resting on this hot summer day in August. Ford, who had purchased the Wayside Inn a year earlier, hosted a picnic for everyone, complete with games and many farming events, Aug. 13.*

LEFT: *Part of the crowd at the Middlesex County Farm Bureau and Extension Service picnic hosted by Ford at the Wayside Inn grounds, August 13.*

best amid midsummer flowers. Woodbine climbed over the roof and golden glow grew against the kitchen wall. Lilacs grew at the corners of the inn and the picnickers found shade under the apple, oak and poplar trees.

The latest addition to the inn at that time was suspended from the corner of the tavern—namely, an exact replica of the original signboard that hung there when the hotel was known as the Red Horse Tavern. On the sign was the likeness of the prancing horse from which the tavern got its name. The dates when members of the Howe family reigned as landlords were inscribed on the signboard. David Howe and his descendants held it in their control for 175 years. The original signboard, enclosed in a glass case, was on exhibit inside the inn. Beside the old sign stood an original grandfather clock. Fitted with new works, it ticked steadily on, keeping perfect time.

The ceilings of the inn were low, balanced by narrow little windows. In an ell on one side of the inn was an old maple table, barren of tablecloth, set with pewter porringers, spoons, knives and forks, illustrating life in Colonial days. In the ell on the opposite side of the house was the public dining room with its fine table covers, silverplated tableware, glassware, china and all conveniences. This was a fine example of life in times long past.

It turned out to be a perfect day for the farmers' picnic—warm, but comfortable. A band concert at 10 a.m. started the program,

BELOW: *A view down one of the rustic rural roads that can be found by compass, but not by road map, between the towns of Woodstock, Vermont, and Concord, New Hampshire.*

which continued throughout the day. While some of the guests were busy inspecting the Wayside Inn, others engaged in horseshoe tournaments, tugs-of-war, baseball games and a parade complete with many floats.

A sight-seeing bus, parked near the picnic games, caught fire in the afternoon, but the fire was extinguished in short order by the Ford emergency fire car. This occasioned temporary excitement, which soon subsided, and the picnic went on.

A report spread through the crowd that Ford was going to make a speech. This drew the visitors to the farm and the truck which served as a speaker's platform. Ford had to force his way through a jam of people, each of whom wished to shake his hand and have a word with him. When he ascended the rostrum the crowd cheered, but broke off at once so as not to miss a word. "I don't know how to make a speech," Ford began, smiling. The crowd cheered encouragingly. "I never made a speech," he began again. "I'm glad to meet you all. I wish that I could shake hands with all of you. I'll circulate around and meet you. We'll do a little farming. We'll restore the old inn. We want to make it pleasant here."

When Ford took possession of the farm at Wayside Inn, it was his intention to help the farming industry in New England through the use of modern farm machinery and methods. At the same time he wished to preserve specimens of old-fashioned farming devices so that the progress of the present over the past might be made clearer. He paid his farmhands four dollars a day—an unprecedented wage—but they worked at something useful every day, rain or shine. In the course of the picnic there were representations of farming as it was carried on in the remote past, the immediate past and the present. On the one side there were oxen that slowly and laboriously trudged along as they drew the plowshare—the way their grandfathers had plowed. On another side were the old reliable plowhorses helping to turn over the furrows—the way their fathers had plowed. And finally a Fordson tractor showed the crowd how plowing was done by up-to-date farmers.

The weather became very warm in the afternoon and Firestone won the applause of the crowd by putting his handkerchief on his head, partially shading himself from the sun. Both Firestone and Ford mingled freely with the farmers and their wives and friends while watching the sports and contests. Of added interest to Firestone were the prize cattle, which he closely scrutinized. Meanwhile, Bill Loring, on behalf of his boys' club at Wayland, Massachusetts, presented Ford with a hoe used in Revolutionary times. "Mr. Ford, I give you this hoe," he began. "It was made by a man named Ben Boyden in 1794. . . ." Ford then broke in and said it was just the hoe he had been looking for all over Michigan. This response made Bill flushed and happy.

ABOVE: *A guest farmer hurriedly moves toward the tractor plowing event at the Wayside Inn picnic for the Middlesex County Farm Bureau.*

When Ford returned to the inn after the reception and his speech to the farmers, he found an old Grand Army veteran awaiting him on the veranda. Although ninety-six years of age, nearly blind and quite feeble, the old soldier, Lewis Seymour, had journeyed the six miles from Marlboro to shake hands with Ford. He had stopped at the inn on his way to enlist in the Union army, and he described the driveway as it was at that time, filled with wagons. Another near-centenarian who met Ford during the day was M. F. Downs of Westford, a ninety-nine-year-old farmer.

It had been hoped that the Edisons would arrive in time for the picnic, but they were unable to start on their journey from New Jersey until the afternoon, and so did not reach the Wayside Inn until late in the evening. Upon arrival, they were assigned to the Edison Room.

On the afternoon of August 15, Benjamin Lovett of Hudson, Massachusetts, an authority on old country dances, called on the party and demonstrated the mazurkas and polkas which were the popular steps in the Revolutionary period. Ford, in particular, was interested in these dances, and so the evenings were spent in dancing the old steps in the inn's old-fashioned ballroom.

Ford valued all the old institutions, including the dance. Subsequently he brought Albert C. Haynes to the inn from Hollywood as dance master. Interest was revived in country dances, such as the quadrilles, the Boston fancy, Fisher's hornpipe and others. Old-time fiddle contests also were sponsored.

On August 17, Russell Firestone left for Plymouth, Vermont, to make arrangements for a meeting between President Calvin Coolidge and the camping party. Russell was fortunate in recognizing several of the Secret Service agents who had been with President

ABOVE: *A close up of a handsome team of oxen that demonstrated early farming methods, August 13.*

ABOVE: *A fine team of workhorses turns over a furrow in a plowing demonstration of farming methods used by our fathers in tilling the land.*

Harding when he joined the camping party in 1921, so he had easy entree into the office of President Coolidge's secretary, Bascom Slemp. The two made plans for the camping party to call on President Coolidge on Tuesday, August 19.

Monday found the party en route again. They arrived in Ludlow, Vermont, twelve miles from Plymouth, before dark and decided to put up at the Okemo Tavern, the local hostelry, for the night.

After dinner Ford and Firestone decided to take a walk, and urged Edison to accompany them. He answered that he preferred to sit in the lobby of the hotel with the other guests and smoke his cigar. After a half-hour walk Ford and Firestone returned to the hotel, and with Edison retired early.

Edison was up at 5 a.m., August 19, pounding on Ford's and Firestone's bedroom doors to arouse them. Ford stifled a yawn, and then appeared in the corridor in his stocking feet in search of hot water to shave with. They all got ready for breakfast and, to Ford's delight, carried whole wheat bread with them into the dining room. This was part of the diet which Ford had prescribed. "My only difficulty, this trip," said Firestone, "is keeping up with Ford's diet!" The diet required strict adherence to such foods as raw vegetables, whole wheat bread and cereals and abstinence from meat.

BELOW: *From oxen, to horses, to the modern Fordson tractor was the theme of the Farm Bureau picnic.*

After breakfast the party enrolled in the Home Town Coolidge Club at Ludlow, and purchased Coolidge campaign buttons from Frank W. Agan and Ernest Moore, former schoolmates of the President. They then got into their cars and drove the twelve miles to Plymouth, Vermont.

Arriving at the Coolidge home in Plymouth about 11 a.m., the guests were welcomed by President and Mrs. Coolidge and the President's father, Colonel John Coolidge. The hosts and their guests made themselves comfortable on the front porch. The President went into the house to get some chairs, then seated himself with Ford and Edison in the Gloucester hammock. After the first salutations were over and everyone had expressed appreciation for the beautiful mountains and glorious weather, the President went to a corner of the porch and picked up an old sap bucket. He returned with it to his seat, and pointed out to Edison the name "J. Coolidge, Plymouth," which had been burned into the bottom.

"I thought perhaps you would like to take it back to the Wayside Inn in Sudbury," the President said to Ford.

Turning to the President, Ford replied, "I never got anything I appreciated so much since I got married."

"It's a sap bucket," Ford explained to Edison, who was evincing curiosity. Although the presentation of the sap bucket began on the porch, the motion-picture operators and cameramen pleaded for the party to come out on the lawn where there was sunlight, and the President assented. The cameramen then asked the party to stand and requested Edison to operate the motion-picture machine.

ABOVE: *Like generations before them, Firestone, Edison and Ford read by the flickering light of the fireplace at Longfellow's Wayside Inn.*

ABOVE: *Ford, the host, welcomes Edison to the Wayside Inn.*

ABOVE: *A view of the entranceway to Longfellow's Wayside Inn, with the cameraman's setup for a photo of the vacation party members.*

ABOVE: *A formal portrait of the group was taken in the Longfellow parlor of the Wayside Inn with, left to right, Mina Edison, Firestone, Edison, Alice Longfellow, Henry and Clara Ford.*

ABOVE: *President Calvin Coolidge stands quietly by as Edison prepares to turn the tables on the press photographers in Plymouth, Vermont.*

222   THE WAYSIDE INN TRIP *A Visit to President Calvin Coolidge*

"Trying to dignify the profession," remarked Coolidge. Ford, meanwhile, noticed a small boy with a camera almost as large as himself, and presented the boy, George Chalmers, twelve, of Rutland, Vermont, with a midget-sized radio watch. "I always carry a stack of these watches to surprise small boys with," he said, "but looking in my grip this morning I found this was the last one left." As the picture-taking session progressed Edison admonished them, "Look pleasant, please."

The President took out a fountain pen and autographed the bottom of the bucket. Mrs. Coolidge, Colonel Coolidge, Ford, Firestone and Edison all signed their names on the bucket, one under the other. The bucket was returned to the President, who wrote on the bottom the following inscription: "Made for and used by John Coolidge, an original settler of Plymouth, who died in 1822. Used also by Calvin Coolidge in the sugar lot when he was a boy at home."

The President explained that the vessel was made in Plymouth for John Coolidge, probably by Lemuel Sumner. "John Coolidge was my grandfather's grandfather," the President said. "He was one of the original settlers here in 1780. It is made of pins, with ash hoops. It will hold about two gallons. How much will it hold, father?" asked the President, turning to Colonel Coolidge. "About sixteen quarts," replied the elder Coolidge.

The reporters now swooped down on the party and asked a number of questions. Edison's retorts were very amusing, and the President and his guests were convulsed with laughter.

"Will Coolidge be elected?" the reporters asked Edison.

"Sure," replied Edison, "if he doesn't talk too much!"

"What is this diet you three are indulging in?" he was asked.

"It's about as much as a cat eats. We have a lot of fun, recalling the days when we could eat ten-penny nails. Now we are obliged to have a particular kind of bread and some of us don't drink coffee, owing to impaired digestion."

"About how many hours of sleep have you been taking?"

"I was up this morning about five o'clock. I'm the fellow in charge of getting the others up." Then he added quickly, "I'm nearly eighty years old. Don't you think I ought to have four or five hours sleep?"

"What about your inventions?" another reporter asked,

"I have several irons in the fire. Now and then I pull out a little one."

After the interviews the party resumed conversations among themselves. Ford reminded Coolidge about the telegram the President had sent him on December 19, 1923, congratulating him on his decision not to run for the presidency. Everyone got quite a chuckle out of that. Firestone then pulled from his pocket a magnificent platinum watch and, turning to Mrs. Coolidge, said, "Henry gave me this one night at his home, when my own had run down."

"You certainly must have been glad to have your own watch run

ABOVE: *A closeup of the maple sap bucket President Coolidge presented to Ford; it was inscribed by each of the vacation party members and later put on display at Longfellow's Wayside Inn.*

BELOW: *Firestone asks Edison, "Are we on the right road?" as they peruse the road map for the way to Ludlow, Vermont, August 18.*

down," commented Mrs. Coolidge. She added jokingly, "I wonder if my timepiece has stopped!" President Coolidge suggested that the party visit the little Plymouth cheese factory, of which Colonel Coolidge was one of four cooperative owners. The party went to the factory, a simple barn structure, and sampled the product in all its stages of manufacture. The cheesemaker was the only person on the payroll, and the four cooperative owners shared the profits in proportion to the amount of milk they brought to the factory for conversion into cheese. President Coolidge gave a thorough description of the process, explaining how much time is required for cheese manufacture and what temperatures are necessary.

When Firestone saw Edison sampling the fresh milk which had been delivered by the farmers to the factory that morning, he expressed considerable surprise. "What!" he exclaimed. "You drinking raw milk? Thought you always boiled yours."

"I do," said Edison. "When I am in a large city. The nearer I get to New York, the more I boil it!"

The party took leave of their hosts and drove to Woodstock, Vermont, where they lunched at the Woodstock Inn. From Woodstock the party headed for Concord, New Hampshire, where they had dinner as planned. Edison did not wish to be guided entirely by maps during the trip, so he used a compass to direct the course of the journey. Here he used a replacement compass, having presented his original compass to Mrs. Coolidge as a gift of the calling party. This method of map and compass took the party over many country roads off the beaten path, and gave them views of some choice New England landscape which they would not otherwise have seen.

After dinner at the Hotel Eagle in Concord, the entourage left for Portsmouth, New Hampshire, where they were welcomed by Mrs. Edison and Mrs. Ford, who had arrived there late in the afternoon on the Ford yacht, the *Sialia*, which had sailed from Marblehead, Massachusetts. The yacht served as their quarters for the night.

On the following morning, August 20, the entire party went ashore, and Ford and Russell Firestone browsed through the antique shops and some of the old houses of Portsmouth, and Ford made several purchases of valuable antiques for the Wayside Inn. Russell attempted to take pictures of jellyfish in the harbor near Memorial Bridge, because Ford had shown a keen interest in these fish.

At 11:30 a.m. the Edisons prepared to leave for the White Mountains and a visit to Bretton Woods, New Hampshire. Firestone and Russell planned to follow, but later decided to visit Exeter, New Hampshire, instead, where Russell had been a student at the Philip Exeter Academy. Ford accompanied the Firestones as far as Exeter and returned to Portsmouth later with them. The Firestones had supper with the Fords aboard the *Sialia*.

The Fords sailed from Portsmouth for Seal Harbor, Maine, to visit their son Edsel and his family at their summer residence. They planned to leave from Seal Harbor for Montreal, Canada, and then go to Detroit via the Great Lakes.

Harvey and Russell Firestone, in the meantime, on a side trip to Mount Washington, struck some bad roads and bad weather before arriving at the Presidential Mountain Range. They took lodging there and planned to stay a couple of days. The next day, August 21, they spent playing golf at a Mount Washington course. A relaxing schedule followed, including some walks and picture-taking of the beautiful surrounding country. Early the next morning, August 22, Harvey and Russell left Mount Washington for Albany, New York, and arrived there in time to catch the train—the Lake Shore Limited—for their home in Akron, Ohio.

On the same day, Mr. and Mrs. Edison arrived at Montpelier, Vermont. They planned to go on to Rutland, Vermont, the following day. Edison spent much of his time studying the possibilities of the country for the development of waterpower. It was not until August 27 that he and Mrs. Edison finally arrived at their West Orange, New Jersey, home.

In actual mileage covered, the camping trip of 1924 was not outstanding. Measured, however, by good times, congenial associations and interesting side trips, the 1924 vacation days rated among the group's best.

ABOVE: *A sleepy New England hamlet similar to many visited on the 1924 vacation trip.*

ABOVE: *Some of the vehicles which brought the vacationers to Plymouth, Vermont, August 19, for a call on President Calvin Coolidge. This group of autos was augmented by those of a horde of reporters and photographers who covered the day's activities.*

ABOVE: *Ford is the focal point of a Concord, New Hampshire crowd, as the party stops for lunch at the Hotel Eagle.*

ABOVE: *L to R: Ken Howard as President Warren G. Harding, Robert Prosky as Thomas Edison, and John Cunningham as Henry Ford in a scene from Mark St. Germain's* Camping With Henry And Tom. *Directed by Paul Lazarus,* Camping With Henry And Tom *opened on February 20, 1995, at the Lucille Lortel Theatre (121 Christopher Street), New York City.* Photo: Joan Marcus.

RIGHT: *Playbill of the play* Camping With Henry And Tom, *featured in Chapter "1921—The President Harding Camp, In The Maryland Mountains."*

By permission of PLAYBILL®. PLAYBILL® is a registered Trademark of PLAYBILL Incorporated, New York, NY.

Epilogue

A nd so the chapters on the various camping trips and wanderings of Henry Ford, Thomas Edison, Harvey Firestone and John Burroughs come to a close. Never again could personages of their stature experience this great land of ours as they had. The vagabonds were older and busier. Apparently, too, the fun was gone because organizing the expedition to include the wives meant a bigger undertaking, while the men preferred the rougher, more informal experience. The novelty of the trips had worn off and publicity had set in. The ever-growing horde of reporters, cameramen and just plain townspeople put an end to this fabulous chapter of Americana.

"The trips were good fun," said Ford afterward, "except that they began to attract too much attention." Firestone perhaps summarized it best with, "we became a kind of traveling circus."

Anyone who has ever taken a motor trip, much less a camping trip, with a party will marvel that the four men, each accustomed to running things, could escape that prime source of potential dissension: the choice of roads along various routes. By common consent the choice was left to Edison, who had provided himself with government maps in addition to the Blue Book. The rest reserved the right to argue at every crossroads. But nobody cherished ill will, even when they got into trouble on the wrong routes.

That was the way these men spent their fortnight at play. When they took off the harness, they took off with it all the trappings. If they were still more or less on parade, it was a penance to them, not a pleasure. As much as they could, they lived simply, wholesomely, naturally. They dealt kindly and generously with one another and with the men and women they met. If it is true that men betray their true selves when they are at play, the record of their various trips and excursions sheds a favorable light on the characters of the famous foursome.

Although the camping compatriots were to see each other many times on various occasions, their wanderings along back roads and their ponderings around campfires had come to a close. A common thread of close personal trust and genuine friendship tied these four men together until their ultimate passing from the American scene.

Bibliography

Books

Barrus, Dr. Clara.
The Life and Letters of John Burroughs. 2 vols.
New York: Houghton Mifflin Co., 1925.

Bloodgood, Dorothy Unruh.
A Postcard Portrait with Memorabilia of John Burroughs.
Bogota, N. J.: Privately published, 1984.

Burroughs, John.
Camping and Tramping with Roosevelt.
Boston and New York: Houghton Mifflin Co.; Cambridge:
Riverside Press, 1907.

Burroughs, Julian.
Recollections of John Burroughs by his Son Julian.
Edited by Elizabeth Burroughs Kelley. West Park, N. Y.:
Riverby Books, 1991.

Firestone, Harvey S.
In Nature's Laboratory.
Akron: Privately published, 1917.

Our Vacation Days of 1918.
Akron: Privately published, 1926.

Firestone, Harvey S., in collaboration with Samuel Crowther.
Men and Rubber: The Story of Business.
New York: Doubleday Page and Co., 1926.

Funkstown, Maryland, 225th Anniversary.
Funkstown: Privately published, 1992.

Kelley, Elizabeth Burroughs.
John Burroughs' Slabsides.
West Park, N. Y.: Riverby Books, 1987.

Marconi, Carole J., in collaboration with Barbara Deveneau.
Longfellow's Wayside Inn.
Historama Booklet. Sudbury, Mass.:
Yankee Colour Corp., 1975.

Muir, John.
The Mountains of California.
New York: Century Co., 1894.

Articles, Periodicals and Manuscripts

Burroughs, John. Journals, 1903-21. Courtesy of Elizabeth
Burroughs Kelley. Special Collections, Vassar College
Libraries, Poughkeepsie, N. Y.

Firestone, Harvey S. Various Manuscripts and Diary
Notes, 1915-24. Firestone Archives, Bierce Library,
University of Akron, Akron, Ohio.

Firestone, Harvey S., Jr. Various Manuscripts and Notes,
1915-24. Firestone Archives, Bierce Library, University of
Akron, Akron, Ohio.

Firestone, Russell. Various Manuscripts and Notes, 1915-
24. Firestone Archives, Bierce Library, University of
Akron, Akron, Ohio.

Huyck, Dorothy Boyle. "Over Hill and Dale with Henry
Ford and Famous Friends."
Smithsonian, vol. 9, no. 3 (June 1978): 88-95.

Keller, Roger. "Civil War Footsteps—Jeb Stuart Appreciates
Funkstown Hospitality."
Maryland Cracker Barrel, vol. 20, no. 5 (1992): 20.

Loskowski, Fred. Reminiscences. Undated. Research
Center, Henry Ford Museum and Greenfield Village,
Dearborn, Mich. Accession no. 65:19.

Leibold, E. G. Telegram to Thomas A. Edison, September
6, 1916. Research Center, Henry Ford Museum and
Greenfield Village, Dearborn, Mich. Accession no. 104: 3.

Mullett, Mary B. "Four Big Men Became Boys Again."
American Magazine (1919).

Index